dwelling

MELISSA MICHAELS

HARVEST HOUSE PUBLISHERS
EUGENE, OREGON

Cover design by Nicole Dougherty

Cover photos © Essem Creatives / Creative Market; vodoleyka, Beautiful_textures / Getty Images

Hand-lettering by Leah Beachy

Published in association with William K. Jensen Literary Agency, 119 Bampton Court, Eugene, Oregon 97404.

Dwelling

Copyright © 2019 by Melissa Michaels
Published by Harvest House Publishers
Eugene, Oregon 97408
www.harvesthousepublishers.com

ISBN 978-0-7369-6319-0 (hardcover)
ISBN 978-0-7369-6320-6 (eBook)

Library of Congress Cataloging-in-Publication Data

Names: Michaels, Melissa, author.
Title: Dwelling / Melissa Michaels.
Description: Eugene : Harvest House Publishers, 2018.
Identifiers: LCCN 2018049636 (print) | LCCN 2018052907 (ebook) | ISBN
    9780736963206 (ebook) | ISBN 9780736963190 (hardcover)
Subjects: LCSH: Home--Religious aspects. | Dwellings--Religious aspects. |
    Self-care, Health. | Simplicity.
Classification: LCC BL588 (ebook) | LCC BL588 .M53 2018 (print) | DDC
    646.7--dc23
LC record available at https://lccn.loc.gov/2018049636

Printed in the United States of America

19 20 21 22 23 24 25 26 27 / VP-SK / 10 9 8 7 6 5 4 3 2 1

contents

Dwelling:
Home + Body

invitation

Feel Well Where You Dwell

Invitation: An action that causes
or encourages something to happen.

Happiness resides not in possessions,
and not in gold; happiness dwells in the soul.
DEMOCRITUS

Welcome, friend.

I'm so happy you're here! If we don't know each other yet, I hope we'll become like long-lost friends as we explore the simple choices and changes we can all make to create a healthy, happy life. As an author for the past 12 years, I've written more than a half dozen books and thousands of blog posts and articles about the home. I've offered countless tips and strategies for creating a home to love. I'm passionate about this because so much of life happens at home!

My philosophy has always been that our dwellings—both our home and body—are intricately connected. Each has the potential to inspire the other to be its very best. Our dwellings will impact our overall wellness and sense of well-being, each like a vessel that can be filled or depleted by our daily choices and habits. The

We can design the whole of our lives to be more beautiful & balanced.

relationship between how we feel, the way we live, and the home we live in is as inspiring as it is important.

The beauty is in the simplicity. We can choose to become more mindful of our daily habits—how we relax and rejuvenate, how we sleep, what we eat, and how well we protect and nourish our home, body, mind, and soul.

You and I will walk this journey together. We'll explore how we can intentionally take simple measures to do immeasurable good for ourselves, our homes, and others. This is our one precious life. Let's live it with care.

FEEL WELL WHERE YOU DWELL

A home is an intimate space where we can create a sense of worth, security, and belonging. It should be the place where we go to feel our best, a haven to recharge and rejuvenate. The commitment to reclaim and refine this sacred space and to protect what we hold dear invites us to make choices that change us, better us, and help us make a positive impact on the world around us. Unlike the well-known slogan for Vegas, what happens in our home *doesn't* stay in our home. The habits and values and forms of beauty we cultivate at home shape our interactions and influence outside the home. And that door opens both ways. What we choose to bring into our home—from food and products to attitudes and design—influences our sanctuary.

If we learn to pay attention to even the smallest details of how we live, we'll discover endless opportunities to better nourish ourselves and the people we love, and we'll be inspired to go into the world to do what we are called to do.

From the moment we wake up until our head hits the pillow at night, we make decisions that can also change how we feel. All aspects of our health are affected, so it's important to become intentional about the spaces we create and the habits we practice. What does that look like? With simple ideas and encouragements, we'll turn intentions into actions. I promise that making the effort to design a whole and healthy life is worth it.

You know those little things that might frustrate you in the course of a day, but you rarely take the time to deal with them? Maybe it's the squeaky bathroom door that irritates you because it invariably wakes up the baby from his slumber, or that overstuffed kitchen drawer you have to wrestle to open every day thanks to the bulky cheese grater that's always been there. Isn't this the story of our life sometimes? We keep doing the thing that causes us stress or makes us not feel our best because it's what we've always done?

Sometimes we become so stuck in how things have always been that we forget each day is the gift of a new beginning. The journey to "dwell well" will reveal gifts of new possibilities. Obviously, removing a cheese grater from a drawer will not fix every challenge we face, but we can still benefit from simple changes in many ways. Daily decisions will add up to the whole of our well-being. So many opportunities to improve and transform the holistic experience of our life are within our grasp. To fuel our pursuit, here are just a few of the healthy steps we can accomplish before we turn the last page:

- We can learn to better care for our home environment, so it nurtures us.

- We can make decisions at home that simplify our lives.

- We can create more peace in our days and in our dwellings.

- We can invest in relationships and expand our circles to feel positive, challenged, and supported.

- We can take little steps toward dreams and goals so we're productive and our passions and callings are inspired.

- We can lean into faith every day for strength and renewal.

- We can make daily, small choices toward greater health and balance.

- We can transform setbacks into self-care invitations.

At the risk of sounding like a late-night TV commercial, I'll just say it: But wait, there's more! So much more. I can't wait for us to go deeper.

THE HEART OF A HOMEBODY

I've always considered myself a homebody, not because I'm a recluse or never leave the house (I do love an adventure!), but because I care about the simple pleasures and activities that center around my home and nurture *all* of me.

> **Homebody**: *One who enjoys the simple pleasures*
> *and activities that center around the home.*

Being referred to as a homebody today isn't what it used to be. Forget the idea of a hermit and think instead of women creating sanctuaries where we can feel our best and be our most authentic selves—body and soul. The proverbial home fires are at the core of our lives, warming and fueling everything we are and everything we want to accomplish, even when we're out in the community and world at large.

The gifts and opportunities of home are more abundant than ever. On a whim you can effortlessly go on virtual adventures around the world without leaving your sofa. Food, clothing, and furniture can be delivered to your door, and entertainment can be streamed right into your living room. You can connect with old and new friends, build your own business, or even clock office hours all from the comforts of home. Staying in is said to be the new going out! Curling up by the fire in cozy pants with a hot cup of tea in your hands is becoming more appealing than a night on the town.

Interestingly, millennials are sometimes referred to as the homebody generation. The lines between where they live, work, and play are becoming more flexible and fluid, integrating all parts of life. What makes an impact on one area makes an impact on the others.

No matter which generation you represent, having the heart of a homebody opens life to what you care about and what will serve your heart, relationships, and purpose. This expansion can start at home. As sappy as it might be, the quote "Home is where our story begins" bears so much truth. So many new beginnings and beautiful experiences can happen at home!

Being a homebody isn't about holing up in your home; it's about becoming whole.

PROGRESS, NOT PERFECTION

Feeling well where you dwell is never about achieving a level of perfection in your home or body. It's about embracing the art of caring for yourself and your surroundings in meaningful ways while growing in grace, understanding, and knowledge along the way. Such an experience calls us to go deeper than a surface survival mode as we explore what *really* matters, what affects our experience negatively or positively, and what nurtures us on the inside and outside.

We all receive daily opportunities to better care for our home and body. If we pay attention to these invitations and respond to them positively, we impact our present and future wellness. Sometimes our invitations arrive in the form of an unexpected crisis or breakdown. While they may throw our home into a tailspin or knock the wind right out of us, these opportunities can also become the catalyst for a fresh perspective or inspire more deliberate changes in how we care for our home, body, mind, and soul.One of my personal invitations to self-care arrived years ago.

Unfortunately, it wasn't the engraved, pretty kind. It was delivered to me through some crazy health issues. And when I say crazy, I mean the kind of stuff you can't even put a finger on to explain. I knew something wasn't right because I felt like a train wreck. Even though I was young and thought I was otherwise healthy, I just didn't feel *well*.

Like many other new moms ready to lose their post-baby weight, I started a diet. The diet plan I signed up for was one of those you hear about all the time on TV, the ones with prepackaged food. The first few weeks, I felt great. The food was good and so easy to prepare, which was exactly what I thought I needed. I was able to work out with a video while my baby napped, so I was feeling stronger too.

But before long I started having symptoms. My heart pounded, and I was dizzy and had trouble catching my breath. I even experienced pains in my chest. My fatigue levels took another dive. I became stressed and anxious. My hormones were all over the place. I couldn't relax or sleep. I had trouble thinking clearly and focusing on simple tasks. I had aches and pains and other random upsets.

My primary doctors didn't have a clear diagnosis other than to suggest my symptoms were either all in my head or the result of being a new mom. They didn't know how to help me except to offer prescriptions that brought on new problems. I was becoming more discouraged by the day.

I knew I was at a crossroads. I have great respect for traditional medicine practitioners; their expertise and intervention have helped me and my family members countless times. However, even in the fog of dwindling health, I received and accepted that invitation to step up to self-care. I became my best—and only— advocate. The first path had little information about what could contribute to my eventual wellness, so I changed direction and visited a naturopathic doctor.

He diagnosed me with conditions no other doctor had recognized in their testing, including thyroid failure. He explained that my body was exhibiting signs of stress overload, which could be complicated not just by chronic stress, but by triggers such as toxins; synthetic ingredients in personal products; diet, food, and environmental sensitivities; lifestyle; and a lack of sleep.

This doctor helped me tremendously! I felt so much better, but regrettably

I couldn't afford to continue visiting his clinic. In the following years I tried to continue many of his recommendations, but I let some of them slide. I started to live with symptoms instead of questioning them. Honestly, I got distracted. I stopped paying attention to how my daily choices might be affecting my health and well-being.

Life grew busy as my husband, Jerry, and I raised our young family, and I put myself on the back burner. This is so easy to do, isn't it? Yet the stress and lack of self-care caught up with me again, resulting in a hard year of depression and debilitating anxiety. I thought I was going to die on numerous occasions.

Nothing says fun date night like your husband calling 911 because you're having a panic attack! Right? I kid, but if you've ever had a panic attack, you know it's no laughing matter. If you haven't had one, I'm glad for you.

That was a low time in my life. But at least one positive lesson came out of that difficult experience: I learned that I needed to allow myself to slow down. *Smell the roses* became my mantra. With medical and family support, and my own determination to manage my health and stress more effectively, I got better!

Yet in the years to come, I still faced seasons with difficult ups and downs in my health and well-being. Lessons kept coming too. A heartbreaking miscarriage, an official diagnosis of hypothyroidism and adrenal failure, and a life-threatening emergency surgery prompted me to look at my health more holistically, as well as to offer myself grace for what is sometimes a difficult journey.

I'm grateful for the invitation I received to care for myself and continue to RSVP! Without those heartbreaking times that revealed how I needed to live differently and more intentionally, I would not have discovered or nurtured the interconnectedness of our two dwellings, home and body. I certainly wouldn't be writing this book or coming alongside you right now without those difficult but blessed times of awareness.

WHAT IS YOUR INVITATION?

Each person has a unique story of how their journey to self-care began. That's why it's so rewarding to share with one another about what we've learned and lost and gathered along the way. So what form did your invitation to self-care take? Was it...

- a difficult health journey of your own?

- a physical struggle someone you care for experienced?

- a season of anxiety or depression?

- a significant change in your job or financial security?

- the loss of a loved one?

- the delay of a long-held dream?

- a year of doubt or hopelessness?

- a physical move that felt like starting over?

- a drop in energy and motivation?

Maybe your invitation was in the form of a positive challenge. Sometimes we commit to greater health because a scheduled special event looms ahead. A high school reunion or a community 10K might shift us toward exercise and healthy eating to be at our best. Sometimes an inspirational story, TV program, or book resonates with us and motivates us to embark on our own transformation.

Even if you can't point to a life-altering moment that inspired you to greater well-being, maybe *this* is your personal invitation.

No matter the current condition of your home or body, you can start today toward a better way. Trust me when I say this: Even a disaster zone can be turned around to become more life-giving and beautiful. I hope you'll be encouraged to know that as messy as the process might look at times, we can always take some actions within our control, leading us toward the life we want to live. Remember, it's about progress, not perfection.

TAKE A BREATH, MAKE A NOTE

To track and celebrate the progress you'll be making, I encourage you to create a journal just for this purpose. Rather than using an electronic device, I suggest you put pen on paper to record your journey to a healthier home and body. As our lives in a digital world have expanded, the slower, hands-on experiences we cultivate help connect us more deeply to our sense of well-being. These days we're all running around at a breakneck pace, and it's no wonder we feel as if our heads are spinning so fast they might nearly pop off. We need to slow it all down to reconnect with what fills us.

Creating lists and jotting down ideas with pen in hand can make us slow down to be more aware of what we really want and need to accomplish. To help you explore this book's material, journaling questions will be sprinkled throughout. I invite you to spend time with these in addition to the end-of-chapter self-care inspirations. My hope is that many of our shared moments will also lead you back to your journal to organize your reflections as you grow in understanding about your home and body, mind, and soul.

The habit of writing down thoughts and questions can become a therapeutic part of the day. Let yourself doodle, ramble, dream. Keep lists and notes. Don't leave the pages blank. Don't be critical of what you put on paper. Just practice feeling joy when you write. Let the pages bring happiness, clarity, and order to your life. Once you experience how valuable this awareness is to your well-being and peace of mind, I think you'll want to keep it up!

Plenty in life can make us feel crazy or defeated, so let's take a different path.

All you really need to start your journal is a simple composition notebook and a pen. Composition notebooks are the same type of notebooks you probably used for Mrs. Peabody's English class back in the day. Remember those? Or maybe your kids have an unused one lying around.

Now, if like me you feel the need to make everything pretty (and maybe even more wildly complicated than necessary, ahem), a humble composition notebook might not seem like enough. I totally get you. But that's why a composition notebook can be so amazing—you can jazz it up however you like.

If it gives you joy, go ahead and get a fancier notebook or all the colored pens. I love to write and sketch with pink, green, or purple pens. Get some stencils to create headings to make your notebook pretty and organized at the same time. Do whatever works best for you, but don't let those creative details hold you up from getting started.

Your only job throughout our entire time together is to uncover and do what works for you personally. You don't have to live your life or design your home like anyone else would, but if you want to feel your very best, you must start somewhere. Use your notebook. Don't leave the pages empty. Fill it up even before you've gathered all of your thoughts. Ask yourself hard questions and be honest with your answers. The key question you can ask yourself throughout this book is also your first journal entry. Here it is:

Dwell Well: What action could you take right now to feel more balanced, to find greater wellness and peace in how you live?

Asking and answering this question through the lens of each topic we explore will leave you hopeful and empowered to take the positive action steps in front of you. No matter our current situation, we can always take steps to find our equilibrium within and improve how we feel. Self-care comes through positive action taken in every aspect of our lives within our control.

SHARING ALONG THE WAY

I truly believe when we learn how to feel well where we dwell, everything changes. Perspective changes, mind-set shifts, and positive action steps toward greater well-being strengthen us for the journey ahead and can bring us greater hope, peace, and happiness.

Whether you're in the depths right now, barely hanging on to hope, or you're doing well and just want to make sure your own home, body, and family stay healthy and happy, I wrote this book for you, friend to friend, from my home to yours.

I'll share my stories, failures, successes, and ongoing efforts to make the most of this one precious life I have. I know you want to do the best you can with yours, too, so let's navigate together. I think the ups and downs and twists and turns of life feel less overwhelming and lonely if friends share the journey with us.

While I don't have everything figured out yet (does anyone?), I have been able to pull myself and my home together a little more every day. I'll open the door to our home and invite you into our story. I pray that something in my journey to well-being will resonate with something in yours, and you'll take away a sense of hope and encouragement.

For better or worse, in sickness or in health, beauty for ashes, I hope traveling together on the journey to self-care will make us stronger. If we were sitting together on a garden bench and snacking from a bowl of freshly picked raspberries, I'd want us to promise each other that, no matter what, this is the beginning of living a more intentional, full, whole, and happy life.

invitation
self-care

- Choose the notebook you plan to use as your Dwell Well journal. Decorate it or add any features helpful to you. Consider numbering the pages of your notebook. You can even leave the first couple of pages blank so you can later use them as a personal table of contents, like a bullet journal. You can fill in the table of contents later as your thoughts begin to unfold. This way you'll be able to organize the flow of subjects you've explored.

- Think back to a time when you felt your healthiest, and then think of a time when you experienced a lack of good health. Consider jotting down why you think you were healthy/unhealthy at that time. What has changed since then?

- What has served as your personal invitation to self-care? Did it take several invitations before you responded with the desire to feel better, live healthier, and invest energy in your well-being?

- Consider partnering with a friend to go through this book. If you do, share about your personal invitation experience and why you're eager for this journey now.

well-being

Commit to Healthy, Happy Choices

Well-being: The state of being comfortable, healthy, or happy.

Wellness: An active process through which people become aware of, and make choices toward, a more successful existence.

Caring deeply about the details of all the aspects of our lives magnifies our pleasurable experiences. Open your heart and your senses to the small things that add grace, ease, and harmony to your living experience now.

ALEXANDRA STODDARD

The chaos of life can make us want to throw our hands into the air, indicating we just don't care about making improvements. But we do care. Deep down we all care deeply about our well-being and our family's well-being.

When we're running out of energy and the stuff in our homes seems to be crowding in on us, we can simply ask, *Is there a better way?*

If you're like me, you struggle with making decisions. Indecision drains our energy and keeps us from moving forward on anything until we can make a perfect decision. Perhaps you're discouraged because your dwellings, home and body, currently resemble necklaces in a jewelry box—chains that have become a tangled-up mess. We don't always know which step will loosen or eventually unravel them, but we can start somewhere.

If it makes you feel any better, I, too, have been in the place where it seemed as if I couldn't possibly unravel the chaos I was in. My home has often reflected how I felt on the inside. I've had to dig my way out of clutter magnified by depressing situations, rebuild relationships while I redesigned my surroundings, and open doors to healthier habits while I removed the junk I had invited into our home.

All along I've had to learn to treat myself better, deal with my own crazy health symptoms, and fight to get well, feel more alive, and be happier. While I've had to face fears and learn to control out-of-control anxiety, simplifying life and creating order around me helped me find beauty again—and feel more equipped to juggle all of the above in the same day, like a boss.

We can trust that each step is getting us closer to where we want to be.

So even though we could become paralyzed by everything that isn't working in our world, let's instead look for ways we can take action and streamline our choices. We can do what we *know* makes a difference. Well-being is a topic near and dear to me. I have felt like a hot mess if there ever was one, but I'm happy to share from my life, because even though I don't have it all together (well-being is a lifelong pursuit), I've discovered many simple ways to improve how I feel.

I'm not claiming I have all the answers to our health challenges. I don't. But I do believe we can simplify the journey. It doesn't have to be as complicated as we often make it out to be, and a sense of purpose and direction alone can be a refreshing change from feeling powerless.

Dwelling: Home + Body

HOME + BODY INVENTORY

We benefit most by paying attention to what we truly need and are trying to accomplish; otherwise, we can sabotage our own well-being. How often do we run out to buy something we believe will improve our life, only to discover it was a waste of money or added to our stress?

Before a designer starts moving your furniture or an architect tears down a wall, they interview you to discover what is and isn't working. They want to know what changes or additions will improve your home. We can start a journey to well-being by doing the same thing. Let's pinpoint areas of your home and life that need improvement for you or the people you love.

 Dwell Well: What keeps you going? List three aspects of your life that motivate you to be healthier and happier. What one area of unease or difficulty cycles through your life over and over?

Read through the following statements and rate them using a 1 to 3 scale based on how truthful and accurate they are for your life right now.

1—Not true at all
2—Sometimes or sort of true
3—Completely true, reflecting my actions or beliefs

____ If I were to say I'm doing really well right now, I would mean it.

____ My home is functional for my life and is a positive setting for my overall well-being.

____ I take time to notice and enjoy the beauty of nature.

____ I make the regular effort to move—walk, run, stretch, do yoga, and so on.

____ I allow myself to rest when I have a break rather than fill that time with a task.

____ Self-care feels like a necessity, not a luxury.

____ I use food to feed and nourish my body instead of to soothe or alter my emotions.

____ Most weeks I schedule time to intentionally nurture physical, emotional, or spiritual health.

____ When faced with a conflict or obstacle, I respond with more faith than anxiety.

____ I build on life lessons and learn from my mistakes.

____ I make appointments and plans that relate to my well-being.

____ During my week, I make time to be in silence (without making mental to-do lists).

____ The feel and function of my home reflect my priorities.

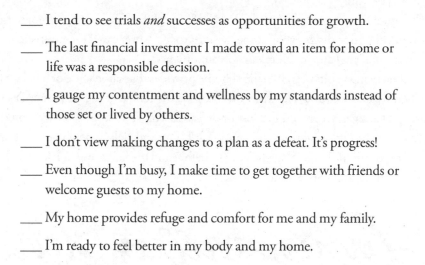

____ I tend to see trials *and* successes as opportunities for growth.

____ The last financial investment I made toward an item for home or life was a responsible decision.

____ I gauge my contentment and wellness by my standards instead of those set or lived by others.

____ I don't view making changes to a plan as a defeat. It's progress!

____ Even though I'm busy, I make time to get together with friends or welcome guests to my home.

____ My home provides refuge and comfort for me and my family.

____ I'm ready to feel better in my body and my home.

First, look at the inventory items you labeled 1. Do they surprise you? Have these areas of your life been consistently less than satisfactory? Now look at those you labeled 2. Are most of them closer to a 1 or a 3? Think through those you labeled 3. Do these stronger areas give you joy? They are likely your foundations for well-being, habits or helps you can draw strength from as you improve other areas during your wellness journey.

If you took this inventory tomorrow, do you think your answers would be the same? Sometimes the chaos or calm of any given day can shift our perspective. However, this inventory and your number 1 and 2 responses provide a good indication of areas you would love to improve, nurture, and change.

THE ART OF WELL-BEING

Simple habits and daily rituals that help us create a space we love to live in can also promote well-being and even greater wellness in the body we dwell in. This is a journey of discovery, so it must begin with a willingness to trust the process.

While we may be able to make a quick change for our body or home and feel better for it, shaping a healthy life happens over time. But don't worry. Simple changes add up quickly and can make a profound difference. With one foot in front of the other, one discovery at a time, we start to feel better cared for, nourished, and more connected and joyful in our surroundings.

Practicing habits of well-being at home provides that same sense of relief we feel when we locate the big red arrow on the directional map at the mall that says YOU ARE HERE. Even when you feel lost or defeated, you at least know where to begin. That's the beauty of starting the journey at home and right where you are. Forget where you aren't. Forget that you've tried before and the habits didn't take. You have all you need to move forward.

Living well is more art than science.

Some changes are easy to implement, and others require some effort and even hard choices. The quest for well-being involves saying no to things that don't serve us well, developing new habits that make us feel better, and being willing to stick with what we know is best for us and our future selves.

Well-being is lifestyle, a mind-set, and a daily commitment to live well through our actions. A one-size-fits-all magic wellness potion doesn't exist. To grow in well-being, we need to become more aware of all the things we do and bring into our home.

We've created a disconnect between how we feel in our home and the choices we make there. Taking care of ourselves often is the opposite of what we've made it to be.

Even if we feel exhausted trying to manage the clutter in our home, we may not remember we brought all of that stuff in there in the first place. We hang on to excess for whatever reason, yet it's the very thing that's making us feel overwhelmed.

We're sick and tired of being sick and tired, yet we don't make the connection between the food we're consuming and how we feel as a result. The food we thought was nourishing our bodies may be making us sick.

Cultivating a sense of well-being in our home is about creating an environment that inspires us to feel better. It's about recognizing the ways we sabotage ourselves from receiving what we really need. It's about caring for ourselves and our families with the simplest actions.

When we embrace well-being as a lifestyle, we realize the full potential and impact of this journey. If we make well-being a side hobby or mere topic of conversation rather than action, changes won't happen, and we won't experience the gift of momentum and positive change. As we take better care of ourselves, our home, and our body, we'll make more discoveries about how we can feel better.

TOSS EXCUSES TO THE CURB

One way to ensure our best chance for improvement is to decide we *are* going to facilitate a change. Sometimes we put up roadblocks to well-being. We say we can't make a change because of whatever excuse we come up with, simply because we don't want to put forth the effort required. Am I right?

And let's face it, sometimes we think we don't have the energy change requires. But I think that's because, when our defenses are down, we believe the little lie that says everything needs to be in place before we can start this or change that to live a healthier life. Does this sound familiar? "If only I had the time, I'd make healthy dinners." "If only I lived in a warmer climate, I'd be out walking every day." "If only I could afford a vacation, I'd be happier."

Self-care isn't something we can do only if we have the ideal circumstances or if we can escape everyday life (although I wouldn't turn down a trip to Hawaii); we can—and must—*incorporate* it into everyday life.

Time after time, I hear people give reasons for why they can't make changes in their homes or habits, even changes that would improve their situation. Now, I'm not saying they aren't sharing genuine issues or valid concerns, but some of these

Health's,
happiness,
joy, and a
sense of
well-being
come from good
daily habits
& wise daily
choices.

reasons are simply excuses that keep them stuck in a constant state of "unwell." (I still make plenty of excuses for why I don't make changes, so I'm not pointing any fingers.)

If we really want to feel better, we must care more about ourselves than we care about trying to protect ourselves from the challenging work of change. Have you made any of these excuses in the past for why you can't make a positive life change?

- I have kids.

- I have cats.

- My husband likes to eat fast food.

- I work outside the home.

- I work at home.

- I have a chronic illness.

- I feel fine.

- My family has a hectic schedule.

- I have food sensitivities.

- I don't have time to research the best option, so I won't start yet.

- I don't have the money. (I spent it on something else.)

- I don't have my own home.

- I'm too tired.

- I'm too busy.

- I work so hard, I deserve to let some things slide.

- I don't understand enough about good nutrition, so for now I'm just going to stick with junk food.

- I hear so many opinions on health that it's difficult to discern what's true.

- I'm addicted to [fill in the blank], and I don't think I want to give it up.

- I can't do this because [fill in the blank].

No matter what excuses have held you back in the past, I hope you'll feel inspired here. Maybe you just feel soul fatigued and need a friend to pull you up, give you a pep talk, and cheer you on. I'm here to help! I want us all to find more joy in the space around us.

 Dwell Well: What excuse has kept you from making progress more than once? Why are you now ready to shed that excuse to gain health in an area of your life?

Whether you're just starting your home and body wellness journey or you're somewhere further on this road, I hope the tips and suggestions in this book will inspire you and even shape your dwellings for years to come. No matter where you've been or what you're facing, I hope you'll feel empowered to take a next step.

START WITH A COMMITMENT

Together, we've pinpointed some strengths and weaknesses, and we've confronted those pesky procrastination and excuse defaults. Now it's time to commit. You can take time with each category of well-being we'll walk through and decide on a step, a change, a goal that suits your needs right now. Even though we'll do this together, our personal versions of progress might be different. We'll never truly feel well where we dwell if we're just trying to measure up to an impossible standard or another person's expectations. Let's commit to make well-being a priority in simple, everyday decisions.

As a homebody and a mama, and along with my husband, I see myself as a gate-keeper for our home. I hope you see how significant your role is in your home too, whether or not you're married or have children. Just as every day we invite things inside for our own good and the good of our people, we keep other things out for the protection of our well-being.

I can't control everything, nor do I need to know everything, but I can be more mindful of what I choose to bring in and diligent about what I know needs to go. Simplifying our choices to what will be good for our homes and our bodies starts with making just one decision—to begin with a commitment to pursuing well-being in our home.

Rather than looking for a quick fix, well-being will become a lifestyle that trans-forms us (and our home) from the inside out. Yes, your mind might be spinning right now with every change you think you should make, or you might feel over-whelmed by everything you think you need to know or understand first.

But let your mind rest.

Just start with a commitment to the atmosphere of well-being you want to cre-ate for you and everyone who lives in your home. Once the commitment is made, the subsequent choices will be easier and even more intuitive as we go along. I promise.

well-being
self-care

- Take a page in your journal, a piece of sketch paper, or a white board and write "Home" on one half and "Body" on the other. List three initial simple steps toward well-being for each side. Your goals might change as we continue the journey, but it's empowering to have a starting place. Read these once a day to keep them on your mind and heart.

- Look back at your Home + Body Inventory results. List the items you labeled with a 1 on a notecard you can carry with you. Use this as motivation to practice self-care in those ways. For example, if you didn't rate high for "The last financial investment I made toward an item for home or life was a responsible decision," this can be motivation to think twice before you hand over your credit card. I, for example, am guilty of buying many pieces of exercise equipment with great intentions, later to realize I use my bike more often for drying out wet towels than to get my heart rate going. A realization like this can be a gentle reminder that you can make whole life, healthy changes with what you already have. Or, find accountability to make better use of the things you buy.

- Share with a good friend what frequent excuse you use to avoid making real changes. If you want to keep this personal for now, write that excuse down and then list several reasons why it isn't helpful or truthful.

- Give yourself something visually satisfying to look at this week while you read this book, write in your journal, or sit in silence. A bouquet of wild flowers, a single tulip, a bowl filled with lemons and limes… whatever makes you feel more alive or inspired by beauty.

- Do you feel ready to begin? Can you let your mind rest and trust that everything doesn't have to change right away? Put self-care and self-grace into action this week in just one specific way. Journal about how you feel after doing this. An example of one action might be to stop replaying a mistake in your mind over and over and instead go for a walk to clear your thoughts, feel better, and be positive. That is well-being in action.

3

sanctuary

Create a Refuge

Sanctuary: A place of refuge or rest.

*I do not understand how anyone can live
without one small place of enchantment to turn to.*
MARJORIE KINNAN RAWLINGS

In this unpredictable world, it's no surprise we need our dwelling to be a soft place to land. We need to be able to turn the key, open the door, and feel warmly welcomed inside. A home should be a comfortable shelter for all who live there, a place where people are refreshed and rejuvenated.

To create a nurturing space, one that treats us kindly, we must become more mindful of the atmosphere that inspires us to feel our best. The choices we make for our home have a profound impact on our mood, health, and emotions. Our environment is like a mirror, reflecting what's going on inside of us, and in turn affects our well-being. If we're discouraged, run down, and haven't cared for ourselves as we should, our home may suffer too. Each crisis we face can add to the chaos around us, complicating how we live and feel.

A home is more than a structure to hold belongings or shelter us from the elements. It's where our very life is lived. It's a place for enriching conversation and celebrations. It's a setting where memories are made, a place to create moments we want to hold sacred. A home becomes the atmosphere where we raise a family and love those with whom we share life.

Transforming our home into a sanctuary where health and restoration are valued and healthy relationships are built transforms us.

Intentionally designing a home that nurtures and inspires the life we want to live is crucial to our well-being. The order and beauty we choose to surround ourselves can be healing to us on many levels. The clutter we're willing to part with, the colors we choose to refresh us, the tactile comforts we select, and the design elements we are inspired by all play a role in our emotional and even physical health.

To rise above the stress around us, we need to create an environment where we can be our most authentic selves.

PREVENTING PILEUPS

Because a home becomes an extension of how we feel, if daily life is chaotic, no wonder our home can highlight that turmoil in clutter and procrastinated projects. When our home is out of control, we feel the frustration. Round and round it goes, right? I'm convinced much of the stress we experience is magnified when we let things pile up. Whether it's the junk we hang on to, or the housekeeping tasks we put off or are unable to manage, or even the wounds we can't (or won't) let go of, pileups weigh heavy on us.

One season I felt particularly in over my head at home. My son, Luke, and my nephew Evan were born just five weeks apart. In addition to my own three kids, I watched Evan on weekdays while his mom was at work. Between keeping up with two preteens and two toddlers, my life, hands, and house were full.

While I adored the kids and really wanted to enjoy homemaking in that season, I just couldn't get in the groove to keep up with the chaos around me. It's embarrassing to admit this now, but maybe you will relate. I dealt with the growing chaos by inadvertently creating more of it.

I didn't realize how counterproductive this was at the time, but when I felt anxious and out of control, I let unnecessary stuff pile up around me to feel in control of *something*.

For starters, I thought it was my duty as the mom to be prepared for almost anything that could possibly happen in the future. I had clothes for kids to grow into five years down the road. I had clothes I might fit into again or wear for a special occasion someday. I saved art supplies just in case someone might need them for a school project. I hoarded craft tools and machines just in case I suddenly found the time, talent, or desire to craft. I held on to items I might want to use to decorate my next house. I never got rid of furniture I wasn't using because I might need it someday if I rearranged the house. I kept items I feared I would regret letting go or wouldn't be able to replace if I gave them away prematurely.

The more stuff I saved for some *future* day, the less I was able to function in the home I was living in currently. The more stuff I saved for someday, the more challenging it was to find anything today. The more piles I had, the more challenging it was to clean the house. The more stuff I had to sort and keep, the more impossible it became to organize what we needed to use day to day.

I let tasks pile up too. I'd save the dishes for later because I didn't want to deal with them. I let the laundry pile up because I was too busy. I procrastinated so long that everything became a monumental task. The more that piled up around me, the more out of control I felt.

Finally, it dawned on me. I was multiplying the chaos, not saving myself from it. I had to stage my own intervention for the good of everyone in our home, especially mine. I didn't hire a housekeeper to do it for me (although reaching out for help can be so beneficial). I decided I had to learn to deal with my own stuff. The pileups had become a weight on me, and I was longing to be free.

I was proficient at procrastinating the process of picking up and putting away physical piles (say that three times fast!). The piles multiplied and became a symbol of my chaos as well as an excuse for why I couldn't keep up.

- Piles of dishes.

- Piles of dirty laundry.

- Piles of clean laundry.

- Piles in my closet.

- Piles of clutter on the kitchen counter.

- Piles of clutter on the kitchen table.

- Piles of bills.

- Piles of papers.

- Piles of stuff to sell.

- Piles of items we might use someday.

- Piles of excuses for why I couldn't deal with the piles.

- Piles of blame for why piles were someone else's problem.

To master all of the piles, I had to let go of fears and counterproductive thinking. I had to stop the pile-up cycle for my own well-being.

- I had to create a home that served my family well in the ages and stages we were in.

- I had to make room for living well now, not find more room for stuff we didn't use.

- I had to take care of the house we lived in, not collect things for a future one.

- I had to learn to deal with tasks decisively and efficiently, not because homemaking was a burden, but because I deserved a home that nourished me and our family.

Don't hate me for saying it, but this new mind-set meant I had to learn to pick up or prevent pileups *every single day*. Yes, every day. Don't confuse this with cleaning everything every day. I still don't clean everything every day. But adopting a few simple housekeeping mind-sets I could practice every day changed my house, and, most of all, changed me. (That said, sometimes pileups happen because we aren't feeling our best. In those seasons, let piles be an opportunity to extend yourself grace.)

DAILY MANTRA

Don't make mountains out of molehills.

When I first started focusing on trying to deal with the pileups, all I could think about was how *hard* it was to keep my house clean! Picking up every day seems like a dreadful process if you're overwhelmed, tired, and busy. It can feel counterintuitive to your happiness, so I totally get it if that's how you're feeling right now.

But that's the thing. When you're busy or tired or overwhelmed, you feel like the last thing you should have to do is clean up piles, so you don't. But by the weekend, the house is a pit, and you're not in the mood to spend your weekend dealing

with it. Four weeks later, you're so overwhelmed you don't know where to begin. A
few months later, you're downright depressed.

Making mountains out of molehills was the cycle I was in until I decided I was
over it. I knew I needed to stop, because the stuff piling up in my house was drag-
ging me down and taking my family down too. My mind-set began to change from
focusing on what I couldn't or wouldn't do to what I could do. Instead of thinking
about what I could save or put off to someday, I started focusing on what I needed
to do today to create more peace around me.

I didn't expect myself to declutter the entire house in one day—that would have
been too much, and trying to take on too much at once is counterproductive to
progress. Instead I zeroed in on what I could do that very day to prevent new pileups from growing and multiplying, saving dealing with the past pileups for later.

Our home and how we feel in it are connected.

I eventually found it rejuvenating to keep things from piling up. I focused first
on the daily pileups that created unnecessary chaos when I let them multiply. The
dishes would have to be washed after dinner, so the sink could be wiped clean. No
more dishes with crusted-on food piling up on the counters! I'd take out the trash
every day, so my house didn't fill up with the smell of diapers or discarded food
(that alone is a psychological boost!). I started doing a load of laundry daily from
start to finish. I made my bed, so it looked too nice to become a dumping ground.
I wouldn't let junk pile up on the entry table, so returning home to a peaceful atmosphere could set the tone for the rest of our home.

Incredibly, the tidier my house became, the better I felt! The less cluttered my house became, the more inspired I was to keep it that way. Preventing piles every day became more therapeutic to me than creating them ever was.

If you don't think preventing piles all day long sounds invigorating, trust me. When I first started cleaning this way every day, I thought I hated this plan too. I remember thinking, *OH MY WORD, I'm cleaning all day long now! Woe is me. Piles are everywhere, all the time!*

But guess what.

Once I got the hang of dealing with piles quickly and decisively, keeping up with my house was no longer overwhelming. I felt so much better because I stopped letting the piles rule how I felt about our home or about myself. I didn't care one bit if I had to pick up ten piles in a day (even if they belonged to someone else in the house) because that was better than letting ten piles multiply into a hundred piles, you know?

It felt so rewarding to prevent the multiplication of piles that it inspired me to avoid creating a pile in the first place by cleaning, decluttering, and tidying immediately. When our daily goal is to just do it and get it done, we no longer procrastinate. It doesn't take much time to clean the kitchen when you do it regularly. Putting away that pile of clutter on your entry table or tossing the piles of shoes into a basket takes only a couple of minutes each day. Running the trash out when the can is full rather than letting it overflow is worth it. Laundry isn't that big of a deal if you do a load every day. You can even fold it while you watch TV!

Dwell Well: Turn to your journal to take notes on your personal pileup hang-ups! What are the daily pileups that happen around your home? Make a list of the areas that become clutter zones, triggering daily stress. What are the tasks you procrastinate doing, eventually creating an overwhelming task for you? What are the pile-up prevention habits you could add to your daily routine? Hang your list where it will remind you to change these habits.

Taking care of our housekeeping piles not only changed how I felt personally, but those new habits changed the atmosphere of our home. It became more peaceful and less frantic. I knew where to find things. I didn't repurchase items we already had. We all began to feel less anxious with less frustration around us.

"Don't make mountains out of molehills" became my daily mantra. It even taught me how to better stop conflicts before they escalated and avoid relationship wounds from piling up.

Even if you feel as if many of the pileups in your home are not your fault, continue to focus on what you can do even if progress seems slow. We can't do much to change others who still want to pile up stuff, but letting resentment or bitterness pile up in us or between us doesn't serve our home well either. You never know. Your new approach could be what changes everything.

DWELLING IN WHITE SPACE

Creating room to breathe in our home is an investment in our emotional well-being. Simplifying our surroundings calms us because clutter complicates everything. When we clear clutter, we let go of a life that no longer serves us so we can have more room for the life we want to live.

Letting go of stuff we really don't need gives us the opportunity to find more joy in the here and now. At first, we might feel awkward saying good-bye to things we've held on to for so long. Perhaps we doubt the emotional benefit of investing so much time taking care of our environment. It's truly a mind-set shift to go from viewing decluttering as a difficult chore to believing creating a peaceful home is a form of self-care.

We may tell ourselves getting new stuff or hanging on to excess stuff will satiate our desire for happiness or comfort, yet those aren't cures for what ails us. We may keep things we don't need, thinking it brings us greater security, or to avoid facing a fear of letting go. We may buy new things to fill a void that can't be filled by more stuff. Buying or keeping stuff we don't need can be a diversion or distraction from self-care, not a real solution for it. More stuff around us tends to magnify our anxiety, not ease it.

Keeping what we *might use* or *could sell* someday won't save us money down the road or bring us peace right now. Storing stuff for a future season that may never come turns our home into a storage unit, which is the opposite of the sanctuary we need.

Surrounding ourselves with excess crowds our ability to find perspective. Overwhelming clutter, noise, and disorganization make it difficult to hear and listen to our own voice. Chaos in our home affects our state of mind and our productivity, making us feel less peaceful and more scattered.

As I learned to stop making so many mountains out of molehills, I discovered my most inspired state of living was "dwelling in white space." That meant I chose simplicity over chaos in my surroundings as much as possible as a form of self-care. I learned to appreciate the feeling of breathing room and peace in my home more than the false sense of control I used to feel in keeping far too much stuff.

Creating white space in your home doesn't mean you have to become a minimalist in style or be surrounded by all white walls if that look doesn't inspire you. Contrary to a sterile existence, for me dwelling in white space means I can live more abundantly in ways that are important to me, undistracted by what overwhelms me.

Having white space in your home and meaningful items around you are not mutually exclusive design statements or experiences. Quite the contrary! The goal is to create an environment where you feel both rejuvenated by your surroundings *and* at peace in it. A home is authentically meaningful when it's more personal.

When your home isn't overwhelmed by clutter, you can feel more inspired by items that help tell your story. Your story is part of who you are. It's the life you live, a compilation of the most inspiring parts of your past, present, and even your future. But if you cannot use, enjoy, or appreciate those items, you need more white space.

What brings you joy? What inspires you to be the best version of yourself? Create an atmosphere that highlights the beauty in your story. Decorating with things we love to create a sense of authenticity doesn't mean we have to fill every corner to the brim. Meaningful treasures can be better appreciated when each item isn't shouting for the spotlight. It's hard to be inspired by our surroundings when we're overwhelmed in them.

Greater well-being often stems from the spaces we allow to be unfilled rather than the ones we fill to overflowing. The white space around what we love leaves us room to grow, breathe, and create. Space is freeing. Clutter is stifling.

Removing trash and clutter (unnecessary stuff) from a room can help ease stress immediately. But anything that becomes visual chaos in a space can distract us from seeing what's important to us, so this process isn't limited to removing trash and clutter.

Perhaps you've hung on to something that holds you back emotionally. Maybe you've kept a design style that doesn't reflect the mood you really want in your space. You may notice things you bought to fill a void but decide that open space is more refreshing to you now. You might have objects no longer inspiring or useful to you, and it's time to let them go.

Once you take the brave step to begin eliminating what you don't need, you'll become more in tune with how other choices in your environment contribute to your well-being. This is where the journey to create a home that makes an impact on you personally will become more meaningful and inspiring.

With more breathing room, you'll better determine what brings you a sense of peace and what doesn't. You'll make better decisions about what to buy because you'll more fully understand what it is you need to feel your best. You may decide buying new things contributes to your stress, as it puts a greater burden on your finances or adds too much visual clutter around you.

As you become ruthless about removing stuff from your home that isn't serving you well, you can begin to pay more attention to what enhances how you feel in your surroundings. You can do so many simple things to improve the atmosphere around you.

Consider the intangible ways your home improves your mood, such as streamlining the color scheme to the hues that make you feel your best. You can enjoy incorporating daily rituals that make you happier at home, such as opening your blinds to let in more sunshine. When your home isn't chaotic, you can enjoy more pleasant experiences there, such as curling up on the couch with a book or playing a game with your kids.

An overstuffed home may inadvertently elevate our stress level as well as create unnecessary work for us. The more stuff we have in our home, the more decisions we're forced to make every day. Excess stuff complicates our life. We have to figure out where to put things we don't have room for. We have to hunt for items buried in chaos. We add financial burdens because we need more space or end up buying the same items again and again because we can't find the ones we already have.

Dwelling in white space allows us to shut out what adds to our feeling of being overwhelmed. Streamlining spaces helps us quiet the chaos and simplify expectations so we can focus on what is essential to well-being.

 Dwell Well: Think about the home you long to live in. What would it feel like to live there? Describe the look and feel of the different spaces. Don't let this become a measure of what you don't have, but rather a reference to inspire your purchases, eliminations, additions, changes, and next steps.

A SENTIMENTAL HOME

What nurtures us at a deep level in our home? What makes your home a reflection of you?

Besides the laughter and presence of the people we love, we can surround ourselves with tangible reminders of all we have to be grateful for. Living with things we love inspires us to view our home as a place where our story matters. What are the moments that speak to us?

The sentimental pieces in our home connect the dots of a well-lived life, heart to soul, past to present, function to beauty.

Paring down excess increases our sense of well-being, but meaningful elements should be among the essentials that remain. Not everything can or should hold space or be put in a place of honor in our home. To avoid the accumulation of clutter, we should keep only what is appreciated and serves a meaningful purpose, lest our home become like a museum rather than a place of life.

My dining table has been in our family since my girls were little. At first it was in our beach house on the Oregon coast, where it became a gathering spot for board games and lazy Saturday morning breakfasts. We eventually hauled it to our new home in Washington. After painting the oak white, it began a new chapter as our family dinner table. We used it as a surface for making gingerbread houses, for making new friends, and for celebrating happy times.

Through the years it's become worn, old, and rickety, but it still serves a meaningful purpose in bringing people together. Will I get a new table at some point? Yes, I know I will. It's increasingly wobbly, and the hinges are becoming more difficult to work with when we want to expand the table to accommodate extended family dinners. Perhaps by the time you read this it will have been replaced, but I don't have any plans at this point either way. Right now, I don't feel a sense of urgency about finding something new.

Certainly, it is important to our well-being to not become overly attached to things, so we need to let go of what we don't need or what no longer inspires us. Yet I think if we rid our home of furniture simply to follow a new design whim or to fulfill our desire to get something new to enjoy, we may discover that, fundamentally, something new doesn't bring us deep, meaningful joy.

It's true we can become inspired by a fresh look (and at times that clean start may be just what we need). I love furnishing my home with something new. But the deepest experiences are discovered through living life and collecting memories. So perhaps in some seasons, the old, like our table, might be exactly what our soul needs.

Filling our home with random purchases won't fulfill us. It's the sentimental memories of times gathered around even an imperfect table that make living so meaningful.

When we recognize the beauty in the perfectly imperfect life we live, even a collection of imperfect or mismatched treasures can spark warmth and happiness. The

Mementos can weave pieces of your life together and highlight moments that matter most to you.

way we design our home should inspire us to make the most of what we have, treasuring the experiences and beauty in our story, past and present.

Before you make major changes to your home, take stock of what's already there. What brings joy? What are the treasures that are useful and connect you to what's meaningful?

Your home becomes a part of who you are. The objects you hold dear can reflect milestones and moments you want to remember.

WHAT TO LET GO, WHAT TO KEEP

Sometimes the things we've gathered bring about mixed emotions. Perhaps they represent a loss or brokenness. While they're still a part of who we've become, often it's best to let those items go if they bring negative feelings to the surface. Why keep things that make us hurt or prevent us from moving forward?

Sometimes objects from a bittersweet season can be gentle reminders to treasure the here and now, because all we have is today. What you keep in your home is a personal choice. Rather than seeing what we keep as merely replaceable accessories to decorate our home, the objects we gather should be tangible and meaningful reflections of special moments in our one-of-a-kind story.

BRING IN THE LIGHT

Lighting is one of the most significant factors in creating a warm and inviting mood. Overhead lights don't create a cozy mood on their own. Natural light is the most soothing, but ambient lighting can bring warmth to dark corners and make any room feel more inviting.

- In the daytime, open your blinds all the way and let as much natural light inside as you can.

- Spend time outside as often as possible, and inside near the windows.

- In the evening, make it part of your wind-down routine to turn on lamps around the house.

- Consider keeping off harsh overhead lights in your bedroom.

- Layers of lighting are the most pleasing. Consider having multiple sources of light in a room, such as a lamp on either side of a bed as well as a table lamp or floor lamp across the room.

- String lights or flickering candles (unscented or even battery operated) add a romantic, cozy glow in any room or even light up a faux or unused fireplace.

- Lighting under cabinets can warm up a kitchen.

- Wall sconces (wired or the plug-in variety) help warm walls and disperse light.

- In the winter, when it's been dark and gray outside a little too long, you may want to investigate a light box for light therapy. Lack of light and sunshine can significantly affect health, happiness, and even productivity.

Your home should nurture you, so it's worthwhile to create the mood that makes you feel truly comfortable!

WE HAVE EVERYTHING WE NEED

As a lover of all things home, I enjoy looking at online real estate ads. Just for fun, I scroll through images of house exteriors and check out the rooms inside. Sometimes I even click on the maps to see the street views and then calculate how far the homes are from mine. Even if I have no intention of moving, looking sometimes makes my mind wander to what it might be like to live somewhere else.

A few years ago, I fell hard for an alpaca farm I found online. Mind you, I've never in my entire life lived on a farm. I truly don't know what came over me… except I do know what came over me. By looking at greener pastures online, I found five acres of them.

The next thing I knew, I was driving with my family to meet the Realtor for a visit. Right at the end of the long driveway was a white farmhouse, just like the one I'd always dreamed about. To the right was a circular drive that led to a beautiful equestrian barn (cue visions of hosting weddings), and then really bringing the entire dream to life, fluffy alpaca ran along the fence to greet us as we pulled onto the property.

In hindsight, I know I need to live on a five-acre alpaca farm like I need to live in outer space. But at the time I let myself envision how I'd look wearing overalls, driving a tractor, and maybe even knitting sweaters from the wool of the alpaca. I didn't even know how to knit, but I would learn!

Praise hands for coming to my senses, or I would surely have been a frazzled and overwhelmed owner of an alpaca farm that I had no business owning. Not that farming would have been a *bad* life—not at all. It could have been amazing! That's part of the problem with being a big dreamer. It's hard sometimes to narrow options when so many opportunities are out there!

I had to come to terms with the fact that harvesting wheat and shearing farm animals wasn't the right life for me (at least in that season—never say never!). Instead, I just enjoy Instagram photos of white farmhouses and alpaca.

> *So much has been given to me I have no time*
> *to ponder over that which has been denied.*
> HELEN KELLER

Though I wish I could say that was the last time I got carried away dreaming about something other than what I have, there was this one shingled beach house.

I must have been born on the wrong coast, because my dream houses always seem to be in Nantucket. But this one was on the correct side of the country! Without missing a beat, I made my family hop on a ferry to look (just in case). Once on land, we rounded a corner and saw it against the horizon, in all its beachy glory, like a beacon of light drawing us in.

We talked about that house all the way home, certain it was our dream come true. Yet as we arrived back in Seattle and walked in the front door of our house, our teen son, Luke (who had been just as excited and ready to buy it as I was hours earlier) said, "You know, we have a good thing going here. I think we can be just as happy staying in this house."

Of course, he was so right. He's a smarty. We already had everything we needed. (Incidentally, I'm still convinced that's meant to be my house; the timing just wasn't right.)

Do you ever think if you just had a more perfect house or different lifestyle, you'd ultimately *feel* better? Maybe you'd be a little bit happier if *this change* or *that adjustment* was possible? I get it. I obviously think about those things too.

Homebodies like me naturally sense the deep emotional connection we can have to where we dwell, so it's understandable that we crave the exact right environment! But don't fret if you're not in your dream house. Experiencing peace and contentment where we live always stems from *what we do with what we have*.

If you have a relatively safe place to live, you have a head start. The design or structure itself doesn't have to speak to every aspect of who you are to be the perfect place for you in any season of life.

LIVING BELOW OUR MEANS

It's true that I'm endlessly inspired by charming home architecture and love to work on the visual and functional aspects of a space. Perhaps you are and do too. Specific homes or features in any house have the potential to add delight or even frustration to daily life, so of course it makes sense when we have the desire or even opportunity to get those details just right.

Designing elements in my own home has been a fulfilling way to nurture my creativity and bring me greater comfort in the home I have. But as meaningful as certain choices can be to those of us who love to bring beauty to a home, having "the right house" or chance to fulfill many of our design whims in it doesn't necessarily afford us what we really need for well-being.

An imperfect home might be perfect for us.

It seems to me that most of us are happiest when we live just below our means. Living on the edge of what we can handle can quickly tip anxiety levels too far. Even though I've admittedly been more comfortable with taking risks and living on the edge with home buying than many people might be, I find this concept fascinating.

What does living below our means look like?

I think it will look different for everyone, so where or how we live is a personal decision.

We can design our own boundary lines for where we live, how we live, and the expenses we want to take on to protect our well-being. Honestly weighing the impact of each decision we make can bring overall balance and harmony.

Choosing a life of simplicity rather than complexity is often the least stressful and most appropriate path to take, no matter where each priority or boundary line falls.

When it comes to our home, it's important to make decisions that nurture us rather than stress us. Even if you have the means to make extensive or extravagant changes in your home or can afford to move to a more lavish neighborhood, you may decide to live more modestly. Someone else may choose to live in a more expensive neighborhood to avoid the traffic to and from work. Two hours gained for their family every day might be worth the additional expense for the peace added to their home.

Likewise, design perfectionists can benefit from setting more conservative boundaries for their home to live below the line of perfection. If you're always feeling the need to improve where you live because what you have or do never feels perfect enough, you may choose to scale back. You may decide what you have is already enough for now, and that you want to invest yourself in other projects.

I love improving my home, of course, yet I'm sometimes slow to make certain changes because I have other priorities in place (or because I have overextended myself or need to bring life into greater balance). Perhaps I've set a financial boundary or want to focus on enhancing our family time instead of getting into a house project. Sometimes a reader of *The Inspired Room* blog questions why I made this or that choice in my home. Because our choices are personal, it's fine to make decisions others don't. We may even make a less than perfect design decision because the imperfect option suits us better in the season of life we're in.

Your home is the haven for what is most precious to you. It isn't a showplace to elevate who you are. Where we live does not define us. Even an unexpected choice can be delightful. We should never feel pressured or tempted to keep up with (or design for) the Joneses or place too high a significance on what others think about our decisions.

Make choices that bring more peace to your life. As you consider the place you call home right now and all of the improvements you'd like to make, what matters most to your present and future well-being is the quality of life you choose and what freedom those choices bring to you and your family.

 Dwell Well: What could living below your means look like? Write down three small steps or choices you want to make during the next 30 days. For fun, ask your family for ideas. List those and vote on the top three.

A healthy sense of well-being doesn't depend on *where* we live or *what we have*, but on *how* we live where we are. We can learn to rise above any less than ideal circumstances to learn how to live more abundantly with what we have. If we can't be happy with what we have today, we'll never be content.

Well-being is ultimately a choice of *how we choose to live now*, not only how we'll live *when* or *if we get*. Of course, nothing is wrong with dreaming about a new home, moving to a new home, wanting to remodel, or shopping for new furniture. Certainly, changes can bring joy, but practicing gratitude for our home changes us.

Instead of dwelling on how the grass might be greener elsewhere, or obsessing over what you don't have that's just outside your reach, what improvements could you make within your means and for right where you are?

What could living below your means change about your life?

Even if your home isn't perfect, in what ways is it perfect for you?

sanctuary
self-care

- *A quick fix*—Do a quick fix of something in your home that has been bothering you lately. A wobbling table? A burnt-out lightbulb? A frame you haven't yet filled with art? Dead batteries in a clock? Take care of one thing today that will make your dwelling a little happier!

- *A clutter-clearing frenzy*—Grab a large bag and set a timer for at least 15 minutes. Now rush around your house with a mission to get rid of hidden excess. Open your clothes closet, your kids' toy box, and kitchen drawers, and toss anything into the bag that's no longer needed. If you haven't used an item in the last 12 months, it should go to someone who will enjoy it. When the timer runs out, head your bag straight out to the car to take to your local donation center. Your home and heart will feel a little bit lighter!

- *A speedy room refresh*—Clear the surfaces of your living room or dining room. Remove all of the piles and wayward items, dust and vacuum, and then put back only what inspires you. Little things make you feel greater peace in your surroundings. Ahh, you and your room will feel so much better.

loveliness

Create Loveliness in Your Dwelling

Loveliness: Having a beauty that appeals
to the heart or mind as well as to the eye.

We are shaped and fashioned by what we love.
JOHANN WOLFGANG VON GOETHE

You may not yet have discovered your inner *joie de vivre* (French for "exuberant enjoyment of life"), but not to worry. You don't have to fly to France to find it. You can find it where you dwell. Even if your existence feels rather ordinary right now, elevating your thoughts or making the most mundane or predictable activities of the day (or even the unexpected events) lovelier can make *anyone* feel a little more uplifted or even spirited.

You might be muttering to yourself right now, saying this *joie de vivre* talk seems a little pie-in-the-sky for those of us who have toilets to clean and laundry to do. I get it. Perhaps you're rolling your eyes because I don't know what you have to deal with. But here's the thing: We all eat, bathe, sleep, work, and relax (or at least we should relax, right?). How we spend our moments is how we live, so introducing more loveliness into our everyday experiences can transform us.

Nobody's life is picture perfect. Nothing will be lovely all the time, so I don't pretend to think surrounding ourselves with a bit of loveliness at home can cure all of life's problems. It doesn't change everything, but I do believe it changes *something*.

Sometimes having *something* you just know to do and look for in every situation is exactly what you need to get through everything. Focusing on living with loveliness day to day gives us the strength and perseverance to find it again in all of the ups and downs and seasons of life.

Beauty can be a balm that soothes the rough edges of life.

LOOKING FOR LOVELINESS

We often need to make do with what we have, yet beauty can be created with whatever tools we've been given. These days many kids get to use iPads in their classroom. When I was a kid—wait for it!—we had an Etch-A-Sketch. But my favorite tool was a box of *fruit-scented markers.* Oh, yeah. Those were the days. Second graders had permission to use the Etch-A-Sketch or markers only on Fridays for the last 30 minutes of school *if* we'd finished our classwork.

Some students chose other activities as their reward on Friday afternoons, but not me. The markers were particularly sacred. As the clock ticked ever so slowly toward 2:15 p.m., I salivated at the mere thought of the joy I'd feel when I got my hands on them. It was downright excruciating trying to focus on a math assignment knowing those fruity delights were waiting. Math has never been my favorite.

Finally, at 2:15 p.m. on the dot, my teacher would give the go-ahead, and I'd make a beeline to the marker station. Watching those intensely vivid colors run across the paper and perfume the air at the same time was pure delight to my senses. I'll never forget the smell of those intoxicating grape and strawberry scents!

Even though I probably would avoid breathing in the fumes of scented markers today, they left a creative mark (pun intended) on me ever since. While I no longer have a teacher offering me magic markers as bait to inspire finishing my schoolwork, now I create motivators for myself.

If I'm having a bad day or feeling stuck in the daily doldrums, I'll search out something to bring beauty back into my soul or to inspire me to carry on with a difficult or dreaded task. Sometimes all I have is the equivalent of an Etch-A-Sketch, but at least that's something, right?

Whether it's a humble vase of flowers in the kitchen that inspires us to clean the counters, or some creative equivalent of scented markers in our hands, we sometimes need a gentle nudge to create more beauty in our surroundings.

 Dwell Well: What is something of beauty that gave you joy during your childhood? Do you still enjoy it? Write about the elements of loveliness you enjoyed during different seasons of your life. What from the early years might you bring back into your days now?

It doesn't take much. Beauty can be a spark that motivates us to create more of it. Daily life can always be made lovelier, even when some parts are *not so lovely*.

We may create beauty to celebrate all the good in our life, and other times we need it because it's all we can do to get our feet to the floor in the morning. Nurturing a beauty-seeking, joy-filled mind-set is so important in all seasons.

Where do you find beauty around you?

YOUR LOVELY LIFE LIST

How we view our surroundings and go about our daily tasks affects how we feel. We're unlikely to be able to change everything (or everyone) in our life, even if we wanted to, but we definitely can be more mindful about how we personally choose to live in our own home.

Philippians 4:8 says, "Whatever is true, whatever is noble, whatever is right, whatever is pure, whatever is lovely, whatever is admirable—if anything is excellent or praiseworthy—think about such things."

If we lived by these words, we could create quite a lovely life, yes? This verse isn't just about positive thinking. If you're practicing the Christian faith, taking this scripture to heart is about cultivating a mind-set that focuses on living out the truth of what you believe. But this verse also implies a healthy life principle anyone can live by. Our thoughts reflect our beliefs, and our beliefs should influence our actions.

Well-being stems from our mind-set, habits, and inner character as well as from our own beliefs and expectations. As we set our minds on creating lovely, admirable, and worthy elements as the foundation for each day, we'll more naturally weed out a lot of junk that doesn't serve us well.

A list of words such as the ones in this verse can be turned into our own lovely life list! Brainstorm attributes, qualities, and specific actions you want to cultivate in your life. A lovely list can help us reshape our thought life, inspiring us to be on the lookout for ways we can redesign and enjoy even the routine parts of our day.

So let's make a lovely life list, shall we?

 Dwell Well: Grab your journal and title a new page "Lovely List." Write out Philippians 4:8 or make a list of your own favorite Bible verses. Use words, quotes, scriptures, or thoughts that can inspire and shape your intentions for the kind of life you want to have and the person you want to be. As you read through your lovely list, let it speak into how you design your days.

DESIGN A LOVELY DAY

What life story do you want to tell through your own creativity? Small details of delight and elements of creative surprise infused into daily experiences can bring more happiness and fulfillment. Don't worry if you aren't feeling qualified or prepared to make life more beautiful in every way. Start by designing a lovelier day for yourself.

How you design your morning will set a trajectory for your day, and you're already designing it whether or not you intended to. Yes, that's right. We already *design* our mornings, even if we default to a morning filled with unnecessary chaos and stress.

Does your morning routine get you where you want to go every day?

Does your morning mind-set serve you well?

Perhaps you haven't really thought about how you experience your mornings. They just happen to you! Or maybe you've always wanted a more productive or inspiring morning routine but just haven't figured out what it should be.

Let's brainstorm ways you might like to start the day. Pour a cup of your favorite coffee or tea and settle in to explore these questions and your answers. These might be eye-opening in a couple of different ways.

- What would your ideal (but feasible) morning routine look like and why?

- What does your *actual* morning routine look like and why?

- What are the excuses or roadblocks you have for why you're unable to enjoy your mornings? (If you aren't sure what happens every morning, it's helpful to keep notes in your journal about where your time goes and what triggers a good or bad morning.)

- What time do you typically wake up? Make note of your internal or alarm clock wake-up time for a week.

- How do you feel when your eyes first open?

- What are your first thoughts?

- What do you do next?

- What are some things that do or don't go well because of your typical morning routine?

- What could you improve with a more inspiring morning schedule?

My mom put our vitamins in the shape of smiley faces on our breakfast plates just because breakfast and vitamins were more fun that way. Infusing more beauty into even small moments sets the course of the day and even becomes embedded in our memory.

My husband, Jerry, is not a morning person. I don't think he even utters a word before noon. He prefers to wake himself up by first motioning our dog, Lily, for a morning kiss (it's quite sweet as it's also her favorite morning ritual). But for quite a few years his next step was to turn on the latest depressing news. The news is not invigorating to me. It drains me. So as soon as he walked out the door to take our son to school, I rushed to turn off the TV.

Silence in my environment is my love language at that hour of the morning. While I have already spoken quite a few words before my husband has even opened his eyes, I still don't like to start my day with a stranger's thoughts or stories filling my head. It's not that I don't care what others think or what's happening in the world. It's just that adding words to the overflow of chatter already in my head creates a jumbled mess I can't unravel, especially before my morning coffee.

I have come to know my own capacity and limitations, and that has helped me greatly in shaping my own mornings. Because I crave that silence, I need to seize the first few fleeting moments of the morning to prepare my mind and emotions for the day.

Once you have a good handle on what happens in your mornings, and what preparation and habits can set the tone for the day you want to have, you'll be able to design a wake-up routine that will inspire you.

4 WAYS TO WAKE UP ON THE RIGHT SIDE OF THE BED

1. Embrace Your Manifesto. What is your daily motto? Write a manifesto you strive to live by. (Example: "Choose Joy.") You could even frame your manifesto for your nightstand so it's the first thing you see when you wake up. Read it to set the course for your day.

2. Reflect on Your Morning Gratitude List. What do you especially want to be grateful for in the morning? What starts your day focused on the blessings in front of you? Turn any usual morning complaints into gratitude.

Make a list in your journal of what you're grateful for. List everything, such as waking up to enjoy another day, your friends and extended family, having a job that provides for your family, having children to care for (even if they kept you up all night!), or your husband (even if he leaves his socks on the floor).

Read through your list every morning before your feet hit the floor.

3. Discover Daily Wisdom with Morning Devotions. Keep a devotional-style book with short entries, an inspirational list of scriptures or ideas (such as your lovely list), or motivating quotes to read by your bed or near a place you create for quiet time, such as a chair in a cozy corner of your bedroom.

If you're accustomed to mindlessly grabbing your phone to catch up on the latest social media drama before you can even see straight, your attitude will welcome this more grace-filled perspective to begin the day.

4. Plan Positive Intentions. As you make your bed or take your shower, focus your thoughts on the uplifting impact you can have on the people you'll see and the places you'll go today. How can you bring a sense of grace and loveliness to your life, home, and the world around you? Jot down a few insights and intentions in your journal.

Dwell Well: What distracts you or derails your intentions and energy? Jot down those things and then list simple habits that will allow you to avoid them. Then you can focus on what matters.

INCORPORATE SCENTS
TO INVIGORATE YOUR MORNINGS

Create uplifting mornings by inhaling your favorite morning scents.

- Brew tea or coffee in the morning and let the scent linger before you take a sip.

- Put clean sheets on your bed.

- Crack open a window and let in the fresh air.

- Set up refreshing essential oil blends in a diffuser:

  » peppermint and lemon

  » bergamot and lime

  » eucalyptus and peppermint

  » orange and lavender

  » grapefruit, ylang-ylang, and lavender

WIND DOWN YOUR DAY

Preparing a gentler wind down to your day can make a significant difference in how relaxed you'll feel when your head hits the pillow. Rather than scurrying about feeling frazzled in the remaining hour before bed, guard that time to indulge in soothing activities that calm your mind.

When my children were little, I craved a quiet evening. They were hard to come by! I'd get the kids in their jammies, help them brush their teeth and get that last sip of water, read stories, sing songs, and, finally, kiss their little heads good night.

The minute I'd plunk myself down on the sofa, ready to put up my feet, I'd hear pajama-footed feet padding down the hall. Night after night I'd try my best to get them to stay in bed, not only so they would get the necessary amount of sleep, but for my own sanity.

I finally realized that to preserve my wind-down time in the evening, I needed to start their nighttime routine earlier. Over a period of a few weeks, we moved dinner a bit earlier, started baths sooner, slowly moved bedtime one hour earlier (new room-darkening shades helped!), and then I had an extra hour after the kids finally dozed off. My plan didn't work perfectly all the time, but it was heaven when it did.

Whether or not you have kids, your own evening routine may need to start earlier than you think! By the time we rush home from work, throw together dinner, tidy the house, or prepare for the next day, we often have little time for ourselves.

What types of activities tend to cause you stress in the evening? Do tensions rise when kids haven't completed their homework? Does a delay in dinner preparation set off a series of stressful events and unhappy people? Do you feel overwhelmed by all the household tasks that don't get done?

 Dwell Well: If your current morning and evening routines feel more like boot camp drills than lovely rituals, write out two lovely practices you want to begin using to wake up and to wind down. We're doing lots of self-exploration in this chapter. If you're getting writer's cramp, invite a friend to go on a walk to talk about ways to welcome stress-reducing practices into your homes.

4 WAYS TO TREAT YOURSELF
KINDLIER IN THE EVENINGS

1. Focus on your essentials. Don't ruin your night with a long list of tasks, but identify what tasks tip your morning over the edge to chaos and take care of them the night before.

Think of evening rituals as self-care, a thoughtful gesture to your future self, the self that will wake up tomorrow feeling cared for!

- Lay out your next day's outfit, right down to your underclothes, shoes, and jewelry.

- Set out a clean towel for your shower (because no one enjoys hunting for one in the chill of the morning).

- Put your coziest slippers by the bed to warm your toes.

- Pack yourself a lunch while you pack the kids' lunchboxes.

- Premeasure the coffee and get it set up in the pot.

- Fill your water bottle and set it by your bed so it will be there when you wake up. (It's a little thing, but it makes me happy every morning.)

2. Reset your kitchen. Give the kitchen a quick cleanup after dinner so you don't create an unnecessary pileup that will cause you future stress. No one likes to wake up to food dried on the dinner plates that are still sitting on the counter. If you don't have time or energy to clean after dinner, get your family on board to help, or, as a gift to yourself, serve dinner 15 minutes earlier to give yourself more of a buffer for cleanup.

3. Prepare a peaceful mood. Before bed, make sure you empty the surface of your nightstand of clutter and grab any piled-up junk, laundry, or other belongings that disrupt the calm atmosphere of your bedroom. Turn on lamps at dusk.

4. Put your mind at ease. Empty your mind of to-do lists and tomorrow's tasks earlier in the evening. Write out plans, lingering thoughts, or nagging reminders so your brain can rest. Brew a cup of tea, turn off stress-inducing TV shows and movies, and avoid scrolling through social media in favor of reading, silence, or your favorite restful music. Experts recommend you stop using electronic screens an hour before bed because the light can affect your quality of sleep. Don't bring work or stressful conversations to the bedroom. Let it be a place where you can enjoy a peaceful atmosphere.

REAL LIFE IS LOVELY

Part of my day as an online creator involves scrolling the internet and contributing to it. Giving some love in the form of a heart on a photo you enjoy on Instagram is spending valuable social media currency. You get to show support, and in return you feel a moment of joy and become part of a community. As Martha Stewart would say, it's a good thing. Or at least it can be good.

Even though we all understand the most magical photos are staged and edited, sharing or discovering that image gives us what we *want* to see. It's maybe even what we think we *need*. Scrolling brings a break from reality and maybe even the hope that these lovely captured moments are out there for us too.

A pretty photo can make time and beauty stand still. It's like art. And honestly, who doesn't enjoy scrolling through Instagram to discover another set of adorable young children perfectly posed at a picnic table, a bouquet of peonies in a sparkling sink, or a fluffy puppy on a front porch?

Moments after I wrote this, I glanced at Instagram and saw a photo of a precious baby in a white farmhouse sink filled with suds and rose petals, with potted plants and lit candles on the counter. Mama's beautifully manicured hand was gently holding the babe's hand. Rainbow bubbles were floating through the air. It was a magical scene so well captured it looked like a magazine cover!

It probably goes without saying, but those beautiful photos are likely artistically staged for our enjoyment as well as the joy of the one sharing a peek of her home, life, or creative expression. If it makes you feel any better, if there are flowers in my sink on a normal day, it's probably after I dumped them out of the vase because the water smelled horrific. Beautiful flowers draped over the edge of my sink are always a sign of a photo shoot.

Yet seeing these idyllic scenes online can make us smile, even if they also make us feel inadequate or potentially become a stumbling block.

A young woman recently shared with me about the discontent that had been growing in her heart for quite some time because of unrealistic expectations set by overconsumption of Instagram. She had started to decorate her home based on what she'd gathered other people would like better. When she decorated with a certain collection of pottery or a certain color scheme, the crowds went wild. If she veered off to do what she really loved, people scrolled past her photos without noticing them. She began creating her home according to what would make her more popular online.

Instagram standards should not be the measuring stick by which we judge how we live. When we enjoy these fairy tale scenes of childhood or pause to delight in the beauty of peonies in a farmhouse sink, let them simply represent what we want ordinary moments to be: beautiful. Yet remember these scenes wouldn't likely be enough to make the crowds go wild without some styling tricks and careful edits.

For better or worse, crafting life into likeable bits of content has become a way of life for many. It's not unusual for people to use an app to create a more picturesque or appealing artistic rendition for what we want our reality to look like. Designing these images is not necessarily a conspiracy to make everyone believe their home is always dreamy or that they live that way all the time!

Even though as a content creator I know these images are often staged for everyone's enjoyment, I still find it difficult to avoid that little bit of discontent and distortion of reality that's inadvertently deposited in my heart and soul. It helps me to remember that these images are the work of an artist, someone who has an eye for creating beauty.

Inspiration seeking can be a welcome distraction from the mundane in our lives, to be sure. Receiving the gift of others' creativity can inspire us to create more of it in our own home. But as with anything that becomes an escape from reality, we should guard ourselves from craving what isn't realistic or meant for us.

As we set down the phone and gaze at our own kids wearing their messy hair and finest hand-me-downs, running through an imperfect kitchen, past that six-day-old droopy, smelly bouquet, we're set up for comparison.

If all the other moms and women can make those magical scenes happen every day, we might conclude that something must be missing in our own life if we can't seem to pull it together for even a hot second. But even if we could, is that the life for us? Would we want to spend our time arranging rose petals for our child's bath, or do we just want to get the baby ready for bed?

While my livelihood and connections are found online, at one point I began to experience what I can only describe as feeling strangely homesick after spending too much time consuming social media. On the surface it didn't make sense. I get to live and work in my home every day! That's good for a homebody, right?

I love what I do. I truly adore the women in my online circles, and I feel so blessed by the heartfelt connections I've made. Finding shared passions and creativity in that common space has been an experience I've never grown tired of. The friendships I've developed are real and perhaps even more warm and welcoming than any neighborhood I've lived in. I've been a part of something I always longed for—a genuine community.

But as the social media channels multiplied over the years, so did the weight of unspoken expectations and the excess inspiration that can stifle one's own creativity. The noise can be almost deafening, particularly for an introvert like me. So as much as I still treasured the community, I began to feel the need to escape from the noise in the online space.

Perhaps it was the mix of consumption and contribution to social media, or the pressure that builds through over-connectedness and the unavoidable sense of

The only way
to find the
fulfillment
we're searching
for is to
fully invest
ourselves in what
is available
to us—the **LIFE**
right in front
of us.

constant comparison, but I missed the quiet sacredness of what it used to feel like to be fully *present* in my own home.

For me to find greater well-being, I had to be content to just *be* home. I had to get my eyes off the computer screen more often and onto the precious people in front of me. I had to shut down the noise, so I could hear my own home speak life and joy. I had to invest my heart and soul in creating the healthy and nurturing atmosphere my family needs rather than worry about whether our experiences generate likes or affirmation from the online space. I feel better when I'm more present, creating beauty in my real life for the people in my real world.

The online world can be too much. Yes, there's inspiration there, but why do we think we need so much of it to be happy, whole, or fulfilled? It's a prescription that doesn't deliver on all of the expectations we have for it. We might feel we need to keep scrolling, perhaps searching for something to inspire us like a lightbulb would illuminate a dark corner. Maybe we keep creating because we think we need to stay in the game for our livelihood. Maybe we're hoping the next reveal will finally affirm our worth, or maybe even answer the questions we're too afraid to ask: Do we matter? Are we even seen? Do we have value?

Just like any activity that keeps us busy, the search for inspiration can be an attempt to fill a void or even dull an ache. Are we missing out on something everyone else is a part of?

The well-being we crave cannot be found without a deeper heart connection to our real world. You may not be as immersed in the online world as I need to be for my work, but you may experience a disconnect from your home in your own way without even realizing it.

Oh, friend, it's so hard to be pulled in every direction, isn't it? It's easy to blame social media, but distractions and diversions can come from anywhere. I think we all feel the pressure when we're trying to juggle too much or look for lovely in all the wrong places. Whether it's keeping busy on things that don't really matter, working too much to try to drown out emptiness, or simply running in circles trying to please or impress everyone, we have to learn when enough is enough.

Perhaps you spend a lot of time at work or watching TV or traveling. Maybe you really don't love where you live, so you've decided it's hopeless to look for well-being there. Maybe you're always on the hunt to find what you sense is *missing*, when the answer to what you're looking for might be in front of you. You can cultivate what you're looking for right there under your own roof.

ADD BEAUTY TO YOUR LIFE

If we aren't fully present to create loveliness in our home, we may not even realize what we're missing. We have to tune out what isn't necessary and what may not be serving us well, so we can discover and find loveliness in what's right in front of us.

Turn On Music for Inspiration

Listen to music that inspires and uplifts while you clean, while you cook, while you get ready for the day. Be observant about how the music affects you. It's not just coincidence if you start to feel a little happier. Music can have a fascinating positive impact on emotions!

Take a Beauty Inspiration Break

Go outside for a 20-minute walk and take note of the budding flowers. Listen to wind rustling the leaves of the trees. Take a deep breath and smell the rain. Feel your feet stepping on the gravel or the pavement or the grass. If it snows where you live, enjoy the fresh, gently falling snowflakes and brisk air. Return home more inspired to create something beautiful.

In the evenings, give yourself a moment or two of pampering. Try a face mask, toss in a bath bomb and relax in a tub, or paint your nails a new color.

Add Seasonal Color

Pick a fresh color for the season and sprinkle it around your home. Small pops of yellow in the spring can feel rejuvenating! Maybe a bouquet of yellow flowers, a decorative pillow, or new napkins for the table. A few simple accessories on the counter, wall, or shelves can bring the new color to your favorite spaces.

Beautify the Heart of Your Home

Because the kitchen is the heart of the home, taking better care of it is a way to nurture your own sense of well-being and personal comfort. But cleaning can also feel like a chore, so elevate the experience by designing more beauty into your kitchen cleaning rituals. Make the experience more pleasurable by pairing the task with something you love or find pleasant. Try lighting a candle or running a diffuser with fresh, clean scents. Perhaps prepare a specialty drink to sip while doing the dishes. Create a kitchen-cleaning playlist you enjoy, or use the time to listen to a new podcast. You could even set up a laptop on the counter and treat yourself to watching a TV series while you wash dishes.

Go through your pantry, refrigerator, and those top cabinets you can barely reach. Toss out the old and clear out the unnecessary. Keep only what you can use and enjoy for the season of the year you're in. Restock your pantry with family favorites and supplies for quick appetizers or meals if you have any occasions with guests on the calendar in the coming weeks. An emergency stash for surprise visits is always a good idea. It's a way to help your future self!

Make Mealtimes Lovelier

Set a pretty table and sit at it, even if just for lunch. Arrange a place setting with a little more care, just as you would enjoy at a nice restaurant. Perhaps even create an Instagram-worthy smoothie! Cut open a grapefruit or a kiwi and notice how remarkably lovely it is. Practice latte art or add cinnamon or nutmeg to your coffee, just because.

Nourishing yourself can boost your mood and your health. Spend an evening with a good cookbook and a notepad for your shopping list. Browsing cookbook images of colorful, beautiful food will not only whet your appetite, but will inspire your ideas for gatherings. An hour with a stack of fun cookbooks or coffee table books can feed your heart, soul, and imagination. What could be lovelier?

BALANCING INNER AND OUTER BEAUTY

Ah, the comparison trap. Just as there is in indulging in all good things, there's always a risk in spending a lot of time taking in the beauty others create. If we allow our inner critic an opportunity to create a mental list of everything we lack by comparison—the money, the style, the clothes, the talent, the home, or whatever it is—our inner selves will fill with undesirables such as envy, discontent, frustration, impatience, sadness, and bitterness. I'm not too proud to admit I have experienced all of those emotions at times.

When we let troubling comparisons fester inside, unchecked and misdirected, those emotions may begin to spill out, turning to criticism of ourselves and others. Insecurity in ourselves can spread ugliness far and wide, which doesn't serve anyone well.

> *Be of good cheer. Do not think of today's failures,*
> *but of the success that may come tomorrow. You*
> *have set yourselves a difficult task, but you will*
> *succeed if you persevere; and you will find a joy in*
> *overcoming obstacles. Remember, no effort that we*
> *make to attain something beautiful is ever lost.*
>
> HELEN KELLER

Loveliness isn't just something we should look for in our physical environment. It's an inner quality we should do our best to nurture. Beauty within is a divine gift we are all worthy to receive; it's not for only a chosen few. It's never divvied out in unequal or unfair measure. It's not offered to divide or shame us. It's like a treasure box, filled uniquely according to our own needs and to benefit our well-being. Don't deny yourself or others this gift!

When we see beauty as the blessing and life-giving opportunity it is, we can't help but want to receive it with greater humility and awe. Focus on the kind of beauty only you can create. The canvas we paint helps us tell our story, reminding us of who we are. We don't have to call ourselves a hot mess or unworthy. We are

Listen to the true longing of your heart, silencing that negative skeptic so you can cultivate what you need to thrive.

creative! Remember that the One who created the most intricate beauty in everything around you also created you. If no one has told you this, I tell you now: You are precious, loved, unique, and absolutely worthy of a lovely life.

Become inspired by others, but then redirect your mind and heart to what is in front of you. We were all created to function at our best with a balance of beauty within us and around us, so guard that gift and nurture it so it always grows from the inside out.

Creating beauty where you dwell should bring out the loveliest parts of you—your heart, your love, your faith, your kindness, your strength, and your perseverance.

FINDING LOVELINESS IN DIFFICULT TIMES

As I was writing this chapter, I received two phone calls, each with heartbreaking news. One young lady nearly lost her life; one young man will have his life taken from him too soon. Both situations and circumstances are tough news to process and almost impossibly hard to face.

Life is so fragile. I literally felt the wind taken from me, and all I could do was be still and cry. I felt too numb to just carry on with my writing as if everything was the same. Everything was different, and the truth was sinking in that nothing would ever be the same again.

All of the emotions I was feeling were trying to sort themselves out, mingling between extreme sadness, utter disbelief, deep pain, and nearly paralyzing fear. I couldn't even think of any words to write. I felt as if I were in a fog. There were no answers to be found. Only questions. I tried to go back to writing, but what-ifs and whys stared back at me.

Would I ever again think that something as seemingly trivial as *infusing loveliness in the day* could help anyone? Where is the loveliness to be found when all you feel is fear and heartache? I started to doubt.

But with my questions came a wave of reassurance and gentle reminders that loveliness isn't to be appreciated only when life is going my way.

The difficulties we think exclude us from belonging to the CLUB OF lovely-life dwellers are the ones that qualify us.

I love these Bible verses: "Consider it pure joy, my brothers and sisters, whenever you face trials of many kinds, because you know that the testing of your faith produces perseverance" (James 1:2-3).

I wasn't in control of the outcomes in either of these precious lives, so leaning into and holding on to what I knew to do brought peace and comfort. I could pray and find strength in my faith and find ways to grow through it.

Difficult circumstances are always reminders to me that all we ever have is *right now*. How we react, respond, and grow is always our choice. We can't necessarily change circumstances, and we may not always be happy with the situation, but we can use all opportunities to develop our character. We choose who we become despite and because of our circumstances. That is the challenge of life—to learn how to cultivate beauty even when it feels as if we're on barren ground.

If everything was always wonderful and the beauty we looked for offered no meaning, we'd become quite shallow people. Heartache can help us care more deeply for others and even live more meaningful lives.

Those moments that rock us to our core offer the opportunity to refocus on what is truly important. Faith is what carries us as we persevere. Life is precious, and moments are fleeting, so why not make the ordinary days at home as beautiful as we can to honor the full spectrum of life?

Soak in beauty around you as a gift when you aren't inspired to create it. If you look out your window, you'll see that life is beautiful. Notice colors in the sunsets, the magnificent light in the sunrise, the shapes of the petals on every type of flower, the black and yellow stripes on a bumblebee, the unique design and scent of every plant and tree outside your door.

loveliness
self-care

- Go on a mental scavenger hunt for a little loveliness in a place you don't expect to find any. Your dreaded morning commute? Your hamper full of dirty laundry? Try to find at least three lovely things!

- Consider how a difficulty in your life expanded your ability to be compassionate or gave you a deeper sense of gratitude for all that is lovely. What do you appreciate about life now that you might not have appreciated before your walk through a harder time?

savoring

Slow Down to Soak Up Joy

Savoring: To delight in.

Joy comes to us in ordinary moments.
We risk missing out when we get too busy
chasing down the extraordinary.

BRENÉ BROWN

When we spend our days rushing to get through them, attempting to fit as much into each hour as we can, or perhaps mindlessly checking our phone over and over as we frantically try to keep up with everything and everyone, it's no wonder we often feel frazzled and disconnected from what is in front of us. We don't take time to notice, let alone savor and appreciate, what we value most.

Our senses are perhaps among the most powerful gifts we have to inspire us to be more present in and observant of our life. When we're mindful of all the sensations and feelings stirred up through the sight, sound, touch, smell, and taste in an experience, we're awakened to the gifts and blessings all around us.

Meaningful experiences become so much more precious when we're as present and connected as we can be. Sometimes that means abandoning the to-do list and schedule entirely to spend time with those we love. Other times it's simply pausing to be aware of the grace in what is in front of us right now.

We can set a mood in our home that nurtures our Mind, Body, and Soul.

Senses alert us to savor the joy found even in the *ordinariness* of an everyday moment. Engaging with our senses as we experience life stirs up a heightened awareness of gratitude. As we open ourselves to fully savor what is meaningful to us, we experience a new level of wonder and awe for living.

Reminiscing about each sense savored in a memory brings back a more vivid recollection. Even everyday routine experiences feel more joy-filled when we recall the sounds, tastes, textures, sights, and scents from each season.

Our senses are a gift to provide us a full, rich life. Everything we need is right in front of us. Be mindful to savor the fullness of the moment so your senses can use it to continue to nourish your soul.

SAVORING THE SEASON

My most familiar family memories begin at home, often triggered in my subconscious as I'm heading into a dark kitchen early on a crisp fall morning. What is it about fall? I've always loved it. Some may mourn the end of summer weather and its adventures, but the following season invites us to savor what it feels like to be *home*, safe and cozy in our own little nest.

The leaves outside begin to turn the glorious shades of autumn, inviting the comfortable rhythms of life to return. A kitchen becomes a relaxed gathering place, a spot where memories are made sacred for the people we love through every transition in life. As I think back through the years with our own kids, each of our kitchens in various houses hold many emotions and moments that have become only dearer with the passage of time.

The return of fall feels almost like the return of an old friend to me. I welcome sights and sounds and scents savored in years past, each stirring up a unique moment in time. I can still hear the sound of my old floppy slippers as I shuffled along the wood floor on those fall mornings. It takes a few blinks for my eyes to focus as I turn on the soft lights over the sink. As my arms wrap my knit sweater tighter, I can't help but shiver in the autumn morning chill right before the warmth of the furnace kicks in.

The aroma of freshly ground coffee wafts through the room, gently nudging me to wake up from my usual 6:00 a.m. fog. A deep breath in and out signals the start of my day; a hot mug warming my cold hands tells me how to savor this season. *Slow down, pay attention, and take it all in.*

Softly whispered prayers invite the sun up as a flurry of children start stirring in the house. With eyes closed, my mind reminds me of the feel of soft baby skin and the sound of tiny slurps from an infant nursing. Fall seasons seem to stitch moments together for me; the thud of a sippy cup hitting a high chair turns into a creak in the floor as a boy in new light-up sneakers runs down the hall.

Morning cereal rings as it falls from the box right after the clang of a spoon hits a bowl. Fridge doors rattle as lunches are packed and kids run off in a mad dash to find lost permission slips in a pile on the table. It's become loud, chaotic. Voices are excited, and the dog is barking. The peaceful mood of the morning turns frenzied.

Homework is signed and hands stuff papers into folders. I will my mind to slow the racing so I can trace the shapes and dimples of all the little hands. I don't want to forget. Colorful bands twist around fingers, and hands smooth a daughter's ponytails with sparkly flower clips. My mind flashes forward to me on her wedding day, clipping white flowers in her hair one last time.

We need to hustle everyone out the door. I hear myself saying it again: *Hurry up or you'll be late!* But I wish I could stop the clock. Backpacks slump on the floor and coat closets are opened. Tangled hangers slow the retrieval of their new winter jackets, and I fit in prayers for the day as arms slide into sleeves.

Blowing kisses from my lips with my hands, my heart savors the small fingers that still slowly curl to wave back to me. If only he'd wave like that forever! Each time I savor it and thank God for the gift of one more wave!

I tenderly whisper *Have a good day, little buddy* over and over to a boy who turns five, eight, ten, twelve. At sixteen I do a double take at the shape of a man taller than me in my doorway, but I say it to him anyway. *You'll always be my little buddy.*

My heart feels as if it's living outside of my body in these three precious gifts. Do they even know how much I love them? Eyes well up, so I blink away tears to repeat it again. *I love you. I don't want you to forget.* They walk out the front door and carpool doors close on repeat until I feel the catch in my breath as young adults climb into the driver's seat. The familiar click of the front door latching behind them has started to slow its rhythm, with two kids out of the nest and just one to go.

The sound of quiet begins to stir up emotions, slowly revealing gathered scents, sounds, touches, and pictures tucked tenderly away in the heart long ago. I see senses as a gift from God to transform me through all seasons. Each is like a little miracle placed within us to reveal the extraordinariness in the ordinary, both in the present and in the future.

Gratefully, even scarcely noticed details, or feelings that could have been missed entirely in the wild throes of daily motherhood, aren't lost. Senses graciously blend present into future, so it all can travel forward with us.

What do we want to take with us into the next season?

 Dwell Well: Take a sentimental journey through some of your life seasons. Write in your journal about the sights, sounds, scents, and textures of different times. What do you want to truly savor from them? The act of journaling about these gifts will help you hold them in your heart to return to again and again.

> *There is a time for everything, and a season*
> *for every activity under the heavens.*
> **ECCLESIASTES 3:1**

SLOWING TO SAVOR SOLITUDE

A quiet reprieve from the chaos of life is so meaningful to our well-being, and a hectic schedule requires balancing busyness with solitude. But how do we find that quiet time for ourselves when expectations constantly swirl around us, distracting us from slowing down to savor life?

- Set appointments to savor your life. Wander alone through an art museum, read a book at a new coffee shop, walk through a botanical garden, listen to music, or even daydream.

- Learn to say no without excuses so you can be more selective in how you spend your day. Guard your time.

- Give yourself permission to live at a different pace from the pace of others around you.

- Create a special place for solitude. Set up a comfortable chair and a basket to gather your books and journals for some quiet time.

- Create rituals reserved for your private time so you look forward to those experiences. Light candles to remind you to stay in the moment, journal your thoughts in pretty notebooks, meditate on gratitude, pray.

- Let some things fall through the cracks so you'll have time for solitude.

- Catch up on emails and social media all in one sitting to avoid their constant interruption to your day.

- Get up a half hour earlier to savor the quiet of the morning.

- Turn off your phone and computer earlier in the evening. The world can wait until tomorrow.

- If you have children living at home, and your husband is home or your kids are old enough to be on their own for a while, shut the door to your bedroom for a short time each day or evening for a few moments of quiet time.

- An evening cup of tea can be a memorable ritual. Slow down enough to savor it in solitude.

- Be yourself and live authentically. Trying to impress is a surefire way to feel unbalanced in life.

THE SENSES AT HOME

How can we savor both the messy ordinary and the joyful abundance always in front of us?

Stirring the senses helps us to more richly experience and reminisce about the comforts of home. Everyone is perhaps more in tune to specific senses, but all can be used to enhance a home or experience.

- Visual people are particularly connected to the mix of color, pattern, shapes, and other delights in a space.

- Some instinctively reach out to touch everything with their hands— they appreciate the variety of touchable materials in a room (hardware, fabrics, flooring, furniture, plants, baskets, and more). Incorporating textures can be important to the sense of comfort found in a space.

- Yet others have a keen sense of smell. Positive memories are often associated with different scents. The smell of lilacs from Grandma's garden or the aroma of the yummy goodness of bread baking in the kitchen can stir up positive emotions that represent home and safety.

- For others, sound is their love language, the way to their heart and soul. They might be inspired by music and their favorite playlists, and soothed by the bubbling of a water fountain, the whir of a fan, or even the sound of a soft gentle breeze blowing through curtains.

- For the foodies out there, gathering around the table for a home-cooked meal full of flavor and quality ingredients can be a source of comfort and delight.

Nothing matters more to our well-being at home than how we feel in it. Incorporating as many senses into our home as we can, can heighten every experience, tucking many away as treasured memories.

Fragrance is the sense most often associated with our memory. A wafting scent through the air can instantly take us back to a moment in time. Infusing our experiences with scents can be a helpful way to create positive association and even an indelible memory of home.

Infuse your home with a scent your family will always associate with pleasant memories.

Create a memorable experience with fragrances through the seasons. I love to plant sweet-smelling vines and flowers just outside the door of our home. In the spring the scent of jasmine, lilacs, and roses drift through the Dutch door in our kitchen. In the fall and winter, I infuse our family's home with happy memories by grinding fresh coffee in the morning, baking family favorites like banana bread, or putting comforting, warm, and woodsy scents in our essential oil diffuser.

Natural scents, without preservatives or fillers that add toxins to the air, are the most beneficial to health and well-being. If anyone in your family struggles with emotions, mental concentration, or even just settling down for homework, you can incorporate essential oils to remind them it's time to be calm and focused. Use scent to be energized for a cleaning frenzy or to relax for sleep.

Make natural linen or room sprays your family will begin to associate with the daily rituals and comforts of home. A purse-sized bottle can hold your own personal blend to carry with you on the go. Spray the scent in a hotel or dorm room for a sweet reminder of home.

Whether you prefer filling your home with the aroma of candles or baking, flowers or essential oils, savor your own signature scents and seasonal blends!

CREATE CREATURE COMFORTS

My husband has found a fair amount of amusement over my nightly winter ritual of being tucked in under a small but exceptionally furry blanket. We live in Seattle, he reasons, not the North Pole. It's the type of fur blanket most people might consider a decorative throw at the end of their bed or one they would love to curl up with while sitting on a sofa. Something so plush and warm might seem a bit overkill for sleeping, but grabbing that blanket as I curl up in bed each night is a comforting experience for me.

It's come to the point where I'm like a two-year-old. I can't imagine going to sleep in the winter without my blankie. I've even considered buying a spare just in case something happens to the one I have. I know. Laugh if you must, but it's super soft and slightly weighted, so it makes me feel extra snug. That's what comfort is all about. When I feel cozy, I can relax better and drift right off to dreamland.

You may have heard the Danish word *hygge* (pronounced HUE-guh). Hygge is about the contentment found in simple pleasures and comforts. It's about savoring all things cozy, such as sipping a cup of hot cocoa by the fire or curling up to read a book under a fuzzy blanket. I certainly have the whole hygge experience down when I grab my blanket at the end of the day.

Long before I ever heard of the word *hygge*, I was fascinated by the impact creating cozy, pleasant experiences in our home had on me. Coincidently, perhaps, a recent study released by Sterling's Best Places named the top three US cities for hygge, and the number one city is—drumroll, please—Seattle.

I'm a longtime Northwest gal currently living in Seattle, so perhaps that explains a thing or two. Those long, dark, gray winters may have inspired me to associate the furry blanket with living my best hygge life.

> *I commend the enjoyment of life, because there is nothing*
> *better for a person under the sun than to eat and drink*
> *and be glad. Then joy will accompany them in their toil*
> *all the days of the life God has given them under the sun.*
>
> ECCLESIASTES 8:15

If you live in a year-around warm climate, furry blankets may not be at the top of your list of creature comforts, and that's okay! Your list doesn't have to include a blanket. Consider what comfort feels like to you and how to create it.

Take a walk around your home. What do you see? To feel truly comforted on every level, we need soft places to land; comfortable places to sit; room to rest, work, and play.

Do you have rooms you pass by because they don't feel inviting?

Does your furniture feel comfortable?

Where do you tend to flop down when you need to relax?

Do you have furniture no one uses or sits on?

Do your rooms feel cozy or cold?

How could you solve any lack of comfort with a simple solution? If we're too quick to reach for our wallets to buy something new, we can begin to see spending money as a requirement for improving well-being. While we certainly can buy new things for comfort, I find it most satisfying to first look around my home for a practical solution.

Perhaps an uncomfortable sofa simply needs an ottoman to prop your feet on or a wide pillow for your back. A seat on a leather sofa we had years ago sloped down so you practically slid to the floor every time you sat there. Adding a board beneath the cushion raised the seat enough to make it perfectly comfortable. Problem solved!

Switching out the legs on a too low or too high chair or ottoman can be an easy solution to discomfort. A pillow on a chair's seat or a stack of books under a monitor can make you eye level with your computer screen.

Pulling furniture closer together in a comfortable arrangement can create more coziness in a large room.

Rugs can soften hard floors and create a more pulled-together destination for comfort.

It's important to create special spots to curl up in, so when you're home everything feels almost right in the world even when it isn't.

Weighted blankets feel like a hug. They may help you or your children relax and sleep better.

If you feel overwhelmed with where to begin to add more comfort to your surroundings, start in a small area. Add more comfort around the chair or sofa where you watch TV, such as a throw pillow, an end table for drinks, or a footstool. Gather firewood for your fireplace. Add cozy shades or curtain panels to warm up cold windows.

If you're ready to make more significant changes to your home, perhaps start with the space you spend the most time in, such as a home office, or the one lacking the most.

CREATE A RELAXING ATMOSPHERE

If our days are spent buzzing about, checking items off our to-do list, and trying to take care of everyone else, the atmosphere we create in our home can be stressful. If we can't relax at home, we need to bring more peace to our surroundings.

Spa Accessories

Soap seems more luxurious when it's in a fancy jar, doesn't it? Incorporating spa-like products in your bathroom will make you feel welcomed and inspired, as if you're on vacation in a luxury hotel. Long-handled back scrubbers, jars of oil-infused Epsom salts, and fluffy white towels and robes can inspire a relaxing soak in the tub.

Soothing Colors

What colors make you feel the most at home, relaxed, and rejuvenated? You might consider neutrals or soft tones the most soothing color scheme, but someone else might feel refreshed with more vivid tones. That's the great thing about designing your own home spa ambience. You're in control. Every mood and season or even the day's weather can inspire you to switch up colors for your own well-being.

Gentle Reminders

We all need those daily reminders to not be anxious, to slow down and savor the life we have, so I find it helpful to spell them out for myself in black and white!

Dwell Well: In your journal, create a list of relaxing words or especially meaningful Bible verses or quotes. Read through your list as needed to refocus your mind and soothe anxieties. Select a few favorites to write separately and pin up around the house as a reminder to be more fully present and savor every moment.

Savor Peaceful Sounds

My favorite peaceful sound at home are the wind chimes outside one of my windows. And I thrive best in a quiet mood, so I prefer hushed voices; soft, soothing music; silenced TVs and computers.

What would be a relaxing soundtrack for your home or quiet time? Does a certain musical artist or type of music soothe you? Do you prefer to hear white noise or the sounds of nature? Set aside an evening to create your ideal spa playlist. Play it to help your mind more fully engage with peaceful activities and moments you want to savor.

My husband and I brought our 50-pound portable boombox with a deluxe set of 20 cassettes featuring nature-inspired sounds with us to the hospital to deliver our first baby. Laugh if you must at the whole cassette and boombox situation, but it was the 1980s, and we thought we were being cutting edge. (If you really want a chuckle, hear this: As we were nearing the baby's due date, we rented a pager for Jerry to take to his college classes with him just in case I needed to make swift contact.)

Restful Rituals

Carve out time every day to relax and treat yourself right. What daily rituals could be incorporated into your day just for you? Preparing a morning cup of tea? Drawing a relaxing bath in the evening? Enjoying a craft? Curling up by the fire with a good book?

Set an appointment with yourself to wind down by doing things you love. Involve as many senses as possible throughout the experience to make it even more enjoyable and memorable.

Refresh and Rejuvenate

It takes much less effort to savor a good meal and be aware of life's simple pleasures when you give your body the fuel it needs to be at its best! Stock your kitchen with quality, nutritious food and make sure you have clear, clean water to drink all day long. Make eating and feeling well as appealing as possible. Shop for fresh organic fruits and vegetables that delight your senses and help heal your body. Keep slices of lemons, limes, or oranges on hand for delicious fruit-infused, spa-inspired water.

STAYING PRESENT IN A MOMENT

Because we're among the first generations to have a cell phone always in hand and social media at our fingertips, we're still awkwardly navigating what this new world means to our well-being.

We can capture every moment and even announce our day-to-day experience at home. What we ate for breakfast, our morning coffee, personal moments, the funny things our kids say, the new pillows on our sofa…it all can be crafted, recorded, shared, and saved.

Creating a life and community through a computer or phone may be becoming normal—or even comfortable. I'm actually in the generation that lived in the middle, with memories spanning two distinct realities of how life can be lived—life before cell phones, and life after cell phones. I remember what it's like to raise kids and live without this technology, and my current existence relies completely on technology for our family's business.

What does incorporating this technology into our lives mean to our well-being now and in the future? Does a cell phone positively or negatively affect our ability to savor what's in front of us? Which life is more full and meaningful—one captured with a cell phone, or one savored only in the moment? It's difficult to draw an honest, uncomplicated conclusion.

Of course, I use a cell phone and social media nearly every day for my own livelihood and community as well as for savoring family memories. They are such valuable tools on so many levels. Yet I still believe that *nothing*, no technology or modern convenience, can ever take the place of what was designed to happen *within* us.

While I'm not entirely sure how to feel about social media, I always come back to these questions: What do we really need for a well-lived life, and what can we do without? Technology or otherwise, I think answering these questions is where the balance lies. We must make choices for what we want to savor every day, or decisions are inadvertently made for us and for those around us.

Don't misunderstand me. It can be meaningful to create content and share glimpses of life through the internet. I love keeping up with friends and family, and I've built wonderful new connections with an incredible community that way. But tools should be just that—tools. Social media and the content created for it cannot become the foundation of our lives. For everyone's well-being, photos created should capture a moment we truly live.

With responsibility, careful execution, and the right perspective, tools can certainly be used to enhance our lives. These same tools can also *distract us* or lure us away from the life we want to live.

Can people live well or even better sharing their lives online without compromising real-life experiences? Of course. I know many do! But many do not. If social media is harming our family in any way, why invite it into our home?

Tapping into social media can become like any other addiction that can take over a life and eventually destroy it, so I don't want to gloss over the risk. We shouldn't fool ourselves. The internet itself is a dangerous place! Inviting social media into our home and opening the door to that world for our children comes with great risk, and it should be considered mindfully and with great care.

For the health and well-being of ourselves and those we love, we need to be aware of the risks of social media and create appropriate boundaries for its use. Social media can feed an ego or trip any of us up with comparison. An obsession with taking a perfect photo can prevent us from fully enjoying a meaningful moment.

If we take care of the moments,
the years will take care of themselves.

MARIA EDGEWORTH

How we choose to live in this modern age must become a conscious choice. These new tools we have in our hand and home, the growing list of apps, the websites, the cameras, the social media sites…do they really bring more happiness, joy, and meaningful connection? And if they do, have we counted the cost? Everything we do with our time and energy comes at a price.

I remember the special occasions when everyone in our family got dressed up and headed to the local photography studio for our annual photo. They were less than stellar experiences, to be honest. At least I can laugh when I look back at the photos. While I still treasure them, of course, I remember full well what led up to setting the stage: the harsh words with my husband as we tried to dress the kids to make it to the appointment on time. Our little ones arriving at the studio cranky and squirmy in uncomfortable clothes. They were probably hungry, tired, and stressed by the new experience, overwhelmed by unrealistic expectations.

Truthfully, I wasn't in fine form. Besides being far too self-conscious about how I looked as a young mama (oh, to look so youthful again!), I worried about how my little cherubs looked. I thought our friends' family photos were always amazing. Their families had coordinating outfits and polished, pulled-together faces. We couldn't afford new clothing, let alone many professional photos, so this was my one shot to make this moment perfect, preserved for all to see.

Yet I felt as if I failed on every front. I gave instructions to small children to sit still and stop crying, my arms grasping for wayward toddlers, bribing kids with stuffed animals so they would pose with fake smiles for another ten minutes. ("Honey, smile with your eyes, not just your lips," I would tell them.)

The photo captured the moment, indeed, including my gritted teeth, their teary eyes, and Jerry grinning through it all. I was annoyed that my husband was able to smile as if he were unaware of the chaos and what I perceived as imperfection. Bless our hearts. We tried. We really did. None of us are immune to the stress involved in attempting to capture what we want to see and preserve it with a camera. Not back then, and not now.

Those images of my family in the photo studio conjure up real memories of that day, to be sure. Gratefully, despite the mishaps, they still captured the faces of my sweet family. Even though the photo shoot was staged, I'm grateful for the effort we made. Live and learn, we always say.

Looking back, if someone had handed me a cell phone, I would have so enjoyed capturing day-to-day life. I can hardly blame any of us for taking advantage of the opportunity. But by incorporating this technology into our lives, are we missing out on fully living in the moments? Are we living our best life? Or are we spending our lives trying to look like we do? Does a camera or the use of social media inspire us to create more vivid memories and even better savor each moment? If we don't know what to do without our cell phone in hand, or we've lost touch with what fuels our soul and fills our self-worth, we've lost something that should be precious to us.

 Dwell Well: What did you used to love doing with your time? What did you lose along the way that you would like to reclaim to savor life? The ability to relax or enjoy a day without an agenda? The gift of being present to a moment rather than feeling pressure to capture it for others to see?

Even under the best of circumstances, I fear that little by little, already we're forgetting what it *feels like* to just soak in what is real in front of us in all its imperfectly unedited and disconnected glory.

If we can't set the phone down for an hour, a day, a week without feeling the impact of withdrawal, that might be a sign we need to do just that—sign off the internet to start savoring our real life.

> *People need to be reminded more often*
> *than they need to be instructed.*
> SAMUEL JOHNSON

MAKE TODAY THE BEST DAY

Life is full of so many moments that *should* be savored. You probably don't need me to tell you that. We all have good days we want to remember and some yesterdays we'd like to forget.

Some situations feel as if they pass in slow motion, yet other hours whirl past us so fast we can't seem to catch our breath before another one begins. Some days can feel exceptionally long and hard, yet in hindsight we see that seasons are over in the blink of an eye.

This, too, shall pass, whatever it is. Some of those feelings may linger, yes. Old wounds, hurts, losses, failures seem to want to stick with us, don't they? As each new season begins, I try my best to hold on to as much of the good as I can. I must be mindful and prayerful about setting certain things aside to have greater compassion on myself, and others, in the present.

So many times I didn't savor what I should have. Seasons of life were often a blur. I fussed and worried when I should have stopped and savored joy. I griped about what I didn't have and pined for what I lost, or I longed for what I hoped would transpire in the next season, wasting precious moments that could have been spent savoring the gifts given today.

We all need to be reminded to be mindful about what it means to really savor life and to look for the gifts in front of us today. It's easy to lose sight of what we treasure in the frantic pace of our modern life.

I'm grateful for grace and senses to inspire me to savor and save the good in front of me right now.

Perhaps, like me, you have so many more vivid memories from your younger years. It's been said that the biggest proportion of recalled memories seem to be concentrated before the age of 30! That may be because so many unique, novel, momentous, or life-changing experiences and occasions happen in those early years. I'm sure it also reflects how fresh minds are when they're young!

Whether you're still living in those years now or they're long past, well-being can be enhanced by making each moment as memorable and special as you can. Even

We
already
have everything
we need to savor
each moment—
Our soul, heart,
mind, senses,
TWO HANDS,
and the people
in front
of us.

ordinary days feel more joyful by engaging our senses, savoring experiences, and looking for the gifts in front of us.

What if we committed to live each day as though it were the very best day of our life? What would we do? What would we savor? How would we be different?

Obviously, we would still have to go about life as usual in many ways. We would likely head to our jobs (or maybe you wouldn't?), clean the house (or not?), fix dinner (or go out!). The laundry pile continues to grow, that's one thing for certain.

But what about each day could be different, or should be different, if we put our heart and soul into living our very best day today?

Every day we have choices. Which feelings do we want to be most mindful of? Which moments will we carry forward? What images, soundtracks, feelings, and scents will we savor, and what memories will they help us hold on to?

I know if today is going to be my very best day, I won't waste a moment of it in regret. I won't stress out about what happened yesterday, because that steals my joy today. But I can worry less and savor more than I did yesterday.

Can any one of you by worrying add
a single hour to your life?
MATTHEW 6:27

Do not worry about tomorrow, for tomorrow will worry
about itself. Each day has enough trouble of its own.
MATTHEW 6:34

Because of the LORD's great love we are not
consumed, for his compassions never fail. They are
new every morning; great is your faithfulness.
LAMENTATIONS 3:22-23

My husband and I have been married for more than 30 years now. In our earlier years together, some days we were too critical, too hurried, and too distracted.

I sometimes wish we could have a do-over, but we're still together and better for it. Moments are more tender for those lessons learned.

We can choose to make today the best day ever.

What if we have another ten thousand days with the people we love? It helps to visualize the future in numbered days. Each one inches us one direction or another, toward savoring moments or wasting our days. Whether we have ten thousand or one, what we savor today is what matters.

TODAY IS THE BEST DAY

Write it on your heart
that every day is the best day in the year.
He is rich who owns the day, and no one owns the day
who allows it to be invaded with fret and anxiety.

Finish every day and be done with it.
You have done what you could.
Some blunders and absurdities, no doubt crept in.
Forget them as soon as you can, tomorrow is a new day;
begin it well and serenely, with too high a spirit
to be cumbered with your old nonsense.

This new day is too dear,
with its hopes and invitations,
to waste a moment on the yesterdays.

RALPH WALDO EMERSON

savoring
self-care

- In your journal, write a list of experiences or moments you would like to savor more.

- Use your phone as a tool to get centered! Set the alarm or appointment reminder to go off once a day with the memo "savor the moment" to remind you to fully *be* in the present.

- Think about this quote from J.R.R. Tolkien: "All we have to decide is what to do with the time that is given to us." So simple yet difficult! Write your first thoughts about what you want to do with the time given to you in this life.

streamlining

Simplify Your Process and Priorities

Streamlining: To make simpler or more efficient.

The sculptor produces the beautiful statue by
chipping away such parts of the marble block as
are not needed—it is a process of elimination.

ELBERT HUBBARD

When we prune down to what is truly valuable to our well-being, we finally appreciate and benefit from what remains.

Do you ever find simple decision making difficult, even when it comes to doing what's best for you? Maybe taking appropriate action toward your goals is more challenging than you think it should be? I know I'm not always as focused, decisive, or disciplined as I know I need to be to succeed. It's been quite a process for me to understand myself and feel motivated to make changes.

It doesn't seem to make much of a difference whether it's food choices, time management, budgeting, selecting a wardrobe, exercising, running a business, goal-setting, or dealing decisively with clutter. I often wrestle with taking decisive action on pretty much everything, equally! When I realized I was having the exact same struggle no matter what I was working on, it was such a helpful insight into an area in which I could grow.

Once you understand yourself better, you're able to learn how to motivate yourself to be more successful or more disciplined so you can make progress in many areas of life.

Here are two strategies I've learned I must adopt to succeed at anything:

1. *Streamlining choices.* As someone who really does want to make the right choice, I feel paralyzed when I'm confronted with too many options. Indecision can be a result of perfectionism. If I can't decide what's my very best next decision, I become a procrastinator.

2. *Setting clear guidelines.* I'm a fairly responsible person, but if there is a loophole or lack of apparent urgency in what needs to happen next, my rebellious side might take over. I might act on impulse and do something unexpected, or even the opposite of what I should do. Basically, I become like a toddler. Heaven help me, in those times I need to come up with firm expectations for myself, or I'll need extra supervision and hand-holding!

Seeking greater wellness requires a commitment to self-discovery and a dedication to self-care. You have to pay attention to how you feel and identify your own weaknesses, so you can learn what you need to do to feel your best. Nevertheless, *knowing* what you need to do and *doing* it are two different beasts! Building the easiest bridge from knowing to doing can inspire our success.

Dwell Well: What two strategies might help you to succeed at most anything? List them and journal about how to apply them to a current situation so you can move forward.

If you aren't sure what is stunting your success, you may want to take a personality test to learn more. *The Four Tendencies,* by Gretchen Rubin, is an interesting book if you'd like to learn more about how you respond to expectations.

We're all unique, so a strategy effective for one person may not make as much sense for another. Just the same, I bet most of us think we'll feel more inspired and confident if we can figure out how to focus consistently on exactly what we need to do. Focus can be a real challenge; we all have so much going on and so many distractions. Simplifying and streamlining everything helps us focus on what's most important to us.

When my kids were little, I often streamlined their choices. They had freedom to make decisions within healthy guidelines.

Do you want broccoli or carrots with dinner tonight?

Over the years I've discovered that to succeed with anything, I almost need to be a parent to myself. Perhaps it sounds silly, but it's a mind-set and system that work for me. No one likes to feel overwhelmed, not even adults! When I set myself up with simple instructions and streamlined options, I not only feel less overwhelmed, but also empowered and inspired.

You have to *want* to take care of yourself to be successful at it, so why make anything more complicated than it needs to be?

ADULTING

My daughter Kylee's most memorable comment as a youngster was, "I'm never tired, and I'm never hungry." She didn't understand that her body needed sleep and fuel to function. As her mama, I had to make sure she got the rest and nutrition she needed to grow and thrive.

Just as I simplified choices and offered help to my three little kids so they could learn to take care of themselves, I'm learning as an adult to offer myself the same kind of TLC.

Most of us reached a point in life when we couldn't wait until we were old enough to take care of ourselves and make all of our own decisions. We all want freedom from rules and expectations! What college student doesn't love the fact that they can finally eat dessert for dinner if they want to? (Okay. I still love that freedom.)

Once we become an adult, though, we realize adulting comes with its own set of rules and responsibilities. We don't necessarily want to pay taxes, show up at our jobs on time, or drive at the best speeds, so rules are set up for us, with consequences

We can THRIVE best when we kick out the junk, live with greater simplicity, and focus on what serves us well.

to encourage us not to rebel against them. We might not like rules, but they keep us in line.

However, since we still have great freedom in other areas of our lives, such as how we get to care for our own home or how we take care of ourselves, some of us struggle in that freedom. We can lack the discipline we need to take care of ourselves as we should.

Even responsible adults make less than ideal choices for themselves at times. I certainly do. Perhaps we rebel because we grow tired of the pressure to keep up with so many expectations, even our own. We can start to feel we deserve things we want even when they're not good for us. Sometimes it's as if I'm silently screaming inside, *Let me live! Give me freedom!* Yet the thing I decide to do with my freedom is counterproductive to my own well-being. You know what I mean?

Perhaps you feel you deserve to have a dietary indulgence even though it's counterproductive to your health or goals.

Or maybe you let your home become a disaster area because you don't feel you should have to be the one to deal with the mess. Or you're just so tired of trying to keep up that you feel as if you deserve to let it go.

Maybe you've decided you're too tired to exercise, so instead you take a nap and still feel sluggish and weak.

Or maybe you run yourself ragged trying to prove your worth, but in the end, all you feel is exhausted.

Whatever it is you do, ask yourself if it's really in your best interest.

Picture yourself when you were a kid. You had to pack a backpack for school, and your mom might have asked you if you had your lunch box and your homework. As you grew older, the backpack seemed to grow fuller, didn't it? Pretty soon you were practically hunched over trying to carry all of your books and assignments.

You can use the backpack illustration as a visual to help you prepare and pack for your wellness journey. You can carry only so many things in your backpack before it's too heavy and starts to slow you down.

What will you need for the trip? You should take what makes you stronger, healthier, happier, and more productive, not what weighs you down, wears you out, and drains the joy and energy from your life.

- We need to have healthy food and water because they help us look better, feel better, and live better.

- We should clear out clutter and junk ingredients because we'll feel so much lighter, healthier, and less stressed when we aren't carrying them with us.

- We should incorporate some form of exercise because we need to keep strong for tough times and be equipped for the life we want to live and the people we take care of.

- We should incorporate what brings us joy and leave enough room for what will bless other people.

Life isn't easy, so choices aren't always simple. Sometimes we have to carry heavy burdens we didn't plan to take with us, yet they become a part of our journey nonetheless. It's also important to leave some room in our pack for the unexpected.

Other times we feel pressure to do things or carry stress on our shoulders that's not ours to carry. When we're trying to maintain an image that's unrealistic for us, trying to meet someone else's expectations, attempting to fix other people's problems, or simply feeling pressured to keep up with our own perfectionist expectations, those are burdens we should set down.

It's okay to say no, or not today, or not in this season.

If we carry everything with us, "just in case" or thinking we can handle it all, we'll eventually feel hunched over by the weight. Carrying too much—especially too much of the wrong stuff—will leave us with compromised emotional well-being and health.

You have to want to take the very best care of yourself, so carry only what you need to be well. No one else will make these decisions for you, but if your choices ultimately compromise your well-being, they will make an impact on the well-being of the people closest to you as well. Make healthy decisions for the good of everyone you love.

 Dwell Well: Look over the list we just went through. Now create a list of what you likely need to remove from your pack and what you want to add to it. Journal about the item that's the most difficult for you to remove from the pack and the one that's most important for you to add during your current season of life.

FIRST THINGS FIRST

What do you need to pick up or set down to feel your best? I don't know what your life is like or what choices will be right or wrong for you, but we're all fighting our own battles and dealing with our own limitations. We must determine what's best for us.

Much like the well-being tip we're taught when we board an airplane with children, as adults we must put on our own oxygen masks first for everyone's sake. Think of it as a moment to rest, to wait, to inhale and exhale, a necessary moment to pause, to pray, and to find greater clarity before you take on another task or shove another worry into your backpack.

Every day we can make decisions that will affect our well-being and that matter to the health of the people we love the most. Days add up over a lifetime, so the decisions we make every single day matter more than we realize.

Carving out the time and necessary support to take care of ourselves helps us focus, think clearly, and be ready to help other people we care about. While adulting is hard for everyone, no doubt, there's really no sense in making everything more challenging than it needs to be. We deserve better than that. We have to grab our own oxygen mask first so we're clearheaded enough to assess what we need to tend to the people we care about.

I remember a moment in my life when it became clear that I had not been putting my oxygen mask on first. My backpack was clearly overflowing with things I shouldn't have been carrying around, and I didn't even notice the impact it was having on my own well-being until it all came crashing down.

The stress and chaos in my outer world began to affect my state of mind. Soon I felt out of control on the inside too. My state of mind then caused more havoc in my outer world until eventually I couldn't hide how I was feeling. One afternoon my husband had to call some friends to tell them we couldn't come to dinner. The reason we weren't going? I was *afraid* to leave the house. As if admitting this to Jerry wasn't humbling enough, I was too stressed out to even call to tell them we were canceling.

You know, I'm more than happy to be called a homebody, but crazy stress in that season of life had brought on frightening panic attacks, which led to a complication of that anxiety called *agoraphobia*. Yep, I literally feared leaving the house.

If I hadn't relearned how to strap that oxygen mask on first, I would have had to trade in my homebody designation to become a card-carrying hermit for life. Admitting the problem is the first step in recovery, as they say, so admitting my inability to leave the house was key.

It's likely that at one point or another you've put your name last on the care list. Why do we do that? Because women are strong, and so we often believe we should feel capable of doing it all. We pride ourselves in our ability to keep all of the plates spinning at once with a smile on our face. And we're often quite successful at that!

Yet what we think is a noteworthy skill can end in a health crisis we probably don't see coming. How could we see it? We can't take our eyes off the plates! We focus on keeping everything spinning, and we get all wobbly and blurry-eyed just trying to stay upright.

The plates we spin don't just represent an out-of-control to-do list. When we try to juggle too much of anything we shouldn't be carrying, it will eventually come crashing down around us, and we'll collapse under the weight. We may even be feeling the impact of things we don't realize we're carrying, like excessive stress, unchecked worries, situations over which we have no control, baggage from the past, or even an overload of toxins complicating our health.

When I suffered with agoraphobia, I couldn't find a sense of well-being even if I wanted to. I couldn't go to a movie theater, go for a walk with my husband, take my kids anywhere, meet friends for coffee, or even visit a hair salon to feel better or relax! I feared situations and places where I knew I'd feel trapped and helpless.

You may not think you're susceptible to breaking under the weight of your backpack. You might be strong and capable. But let me tell you the truth. A state of being "unwell" can and will sneak up on you if you're not careful. The decisions you make without thinking every day, the choices that aren't serving you well, add up.

Putting on your oxygen mask makes everything else you need to do less complicated. It simplifies your life and gives your mind, body, and soul what they need to thrive.

So first things first. Strap on that oxygen mask, friend, and let's do this.

TAKE CARE OF YOUR FUTURE SELF TOO

Recently, the electrical power in our house went off after a big gust of wind swept through the trees. I was so cozy in my bed at that moment that all I wanted to do was pull the covers over my head and stay there all day. I had been working for several weeks straight on some hard deadlines, so I was extra tired and worn out.

Yet even though it was Saturday, I needed to get up and get working. *No rest for the weary*, I told myself! When you're self-employed, the days of the week don't have as much significance as pressing deadlines. I absolutely love the freedom of owning my own business, and I wouldn't change my usual schedule for the world, but now and then the associated responsibilities put a damper on weekends.

The rest of the family, on the other hand, was taking full advantage of a lazy Saturday without electricity. They decided to drive to a local restaurant and order blueberry pancakes to go. All my husband had to do was utter the word *pancakes*, and my mind instantly drifted to memories of many relaxing Saturday mornings in years gone by. *Lazy Saturdays and pancakes go together,* I told myself. *You deserve pancakes.* Even though I *knew* a stack of pancakes would not make me feel good in the long run—instead they would probably make me feel crummy—I heard myself saying something along the lines of "Gimme all the pancakes."

Don't get me wrong. They tasted great. But obviously, what I really needed was the lazy Saturday, not the pancakes. Sigh. Eating the pancakes made me feel momentarily as if I had solved the problem, but that didn't get to the core issue. My body and mind were crying out for rest and time off.

I had learned to impulsively grab a "fix" whenever I felt nervous, anxious, tired, insecure, or depressed. Maybe chocolate. Perhaps something new, such as another throw pillow to add to my collection. I think one could determine my state of mind by the number of pillows piled up in my garage.

Whatever that fix is, it's instinctive for many of us. If we try to soothe our way to well-being, we don't always think about what will serve our future self well. What I've now learned I need to do in those moments is consider my physical and emotional *needs*. It's a mind-set shift. I deserve to truly be taken care of, and so I do.

Making a shift from mindlessly appeasing myself with whatever I can grab to soothe feelings in the moment, to giving myself what fills my heart, soul, and mind, has been a process. I had to become a student of my own behavior and needs. That's hard for those of us who spend most of our days taking care of everyone else, isn't it?

Even though I'm still in process in so many areas of life, I cannot tell you what a relief it is to finally know it's important to have greater *awareness* of what I need. Seeking more awareness is what propels me to know how to take better care of myself now, but best of all I'm investing in the care of my future self too.

When we don't consider our future selves, it's especially challenging to make better choices because we can't see an immediate or noticeable connection between our choices and how they make us feel.

Nibbling on one vegetable won't necessarily make a significant difference in how we feel physically or what we look like later today. Exchanging French fries for broccoli is a step in the right direction, of course, but it's an easy step to put off taking until tomorrow. If I give myself a choice between fries and broccoli, I'm pretty sure fries will win every time.

If you have an allergy to cats, like my husband does, you probably get all sneezy

A lifestyle
of
well-being
becomes
effective
when we take
care of
ourselves
on a
continuous,
not momentary,
basis.

around felines. That provides clear and immediate consequence. You know with 100 percent certainty that it's not ideal to pet a cat because sneezing will occur. You probably avoid cats. Well, you might choose to pet a cat anyway simply because you find joy in fluffing their furry faces. That's understandable, but at least you know to be prepared for feeling miserable later.

When we prioritize truly caring for our own needs, the other decisions in our day tend to become easier in time. Whether we choose broccoli or fries with lunch today, cats with a side of sneezing in the afternoon, or pancakes when we really just need a day off, all of our choices matter cumulatively. But none are as life-altering as the decision to first be true to ourselves, so we can provide what we need to feel our best.

We can't control many things, it's true, but we can be more mindful of the choices we make. We can decide how well we'll nurture ourselves in this season and beyond, no matter what's going on around us. Caring for ourselves is about making choices we believe will be best for us, even when no one is around to know what choice we made, simply because we deserve to be well.

As we learn our own strengths and weaknesses, we can begin the process of taking better care of ourselves and improving how we feel inside and out.

PAYING ATTENTION TO
WHAT'S IN FRONT OF US

A couple of winters ago I experienced a calamity involving my feet and an unexpected patch of ice. I was walking to a local coffee shop with my daughter, commenting on her super cute boots. The next thing I knew, *BAM!* I was flying through the air toward the ground, arms flailing every which way, legs doing the splits (honestly, I didn't even know I could still do those!). All the while Courtney was looking at me in shock and horror from a few feet away.

As I was making my painfully slow and embarrassing descent toward the cold hard pavement, it was clear there was no way to stop the impending collision.

I spent what was perhaps the longest split second of my life trying to think of anything I could do to break my fall and avoid the ice. But I had nothing to grab to slow myself down. When your hands and feet can't find anything solid to grip, you're going down, and it isn't going to be graceful.

Fortunately, I didn't hit my head, lose consciousness, or break any bones. After I made contact with the ice, I could move all my extremities (even though I could tell my knees and hands were bruised and sprained), but I *could not* get up off that ice for a good three minutes. I laughed the entire time and was *so* grateful only my daughter was there to witness it all.

Now, mind you, as if that icy fall wasn't traumatizing enough, it took place just two days after a milestone birthday—one of those birthdays when you can't believe you're "that old." Nothing like a fall on the ice to remind you that you aren't as young as you used to be.

The good news is that fall on the ice reminded me of a valuable lesson for wellness. To be well, we have to pay close attention to what's right in front of us. We don't have to live in fear of living life. We just have to live in greater mindfulness and awareness of how we feel.

Training your mind to pay closer attention to the next step in front of you not only can make you feel better, but it can help you avoid decisions that cause you more harm than good.

GARBAGE IN, GARBAGE OUT

Have you heard of the computer programming concept "garbage in, garbage out"? No doubt, if we put toxins in our mouth or on our skin or use products filled with junk, we're going to start to feel like garbage. Whether with an immediate reaction or one we experience down the road, our health and well-being will be affected by our choices today. It's a guarantee.

Nearly 30 years ago, when I was first diagnosed with hypothyroidism and adrenal failure, my naturopathic doctor explained that the systems in my body were being worn down by stress and the toxic overload of products I had brought into my home.

Say what? I was in my early twenties and trying to take care of myself, or so I thought. Wasn't I too young to be worn down? It was an eye-opening and sobering revelation.

I'm so grateful for that doctor, because he made me more aware of the havoc that even common or so-called "healthy" food items or products can wreak in our bodies. I've carried that awareness with me ever since. Awareness doesn't mean I always get it right, but it inspires me to pay closer attention when something seems amiss.

About a decade later, when our now nearly 19-year-old son was a little over a year old, he started exhibiting a few unusual symptoms over a period of several weeks. Luke had gone from a generally happy, contented, breastfed baby to being prone to outbursts of extreme sadness and tantrums. He also had some noticeable digestive upsets, but the most prominent symptom appeared to be emotional.

It broke my heart to see my little buddy suffering. He would sit in his high chair and cry uncontrollably after a meal. I'd wrap my arms around his head to comfort him and quietly sob myself. What was happening to make him so miserable?

When we went to his pediatrician to rule out anything obvious, I mentioned the possibility of it being a reaction to food. My son was at the age when babies are transitioning to regular table foods, so a lightbulb was going off inside my head. But I was met with a familiar blank stare I had seen from doctors when they'd considered my own weird symptoms.

Again, I was grateful my naturopathic doctor had encouraged me to consider the food we eat and the products we bring into our home as potential triggers for health symptoms. Armed with that possibility in my son's situation, I knew where to start. While no answers were coming from my pediatrician's office, I wasn't going to take "there's nothing wrong" for an answer. Without question I would be Luke's wellness advocate and do everything and anything I could to find a solution.

Tears are flowing again as I write this, just remembering how I felt to be a mama with a hurting child. It was one thing for me to suffer mysterious ailments as an adult, and another for my baby! My heart hurts for mamas who go through difficulties with a baby's health when, after the all-important first steps of prayer and exercising faith, there doesn't seem to be a clear or obvious next step they can take.

Because the connection to food felt so possible in my son's situation, I started to diligently scour books, study labels, and eliminate anything from his diet that seemed to stir up symptoms. Sugar, cow's milk (including casein), synthetic dyes, and preservatives were clearly connected. I even tossed out items labeled "natural" or "recommended for a healthy diet" if they didn't agree with him.

While the connection between health problems, food, and environment is better researched than ever before, and trusted information is so much more available than when I was a young mom, we still have to do our research and become our own advocates when it comes to how we feel.

It's still not as widely intuitive as it should be to connect symptoms to food or treat health conditions with environmental changes. I don't think we fully comprehend the magnitude of the problem in our environment, or the potential ease with which we may be able to resolve or even reverse some conditions by simple changes to diet and household habits.

It's worth looking for ways to alter diet and environment as a means to potentially feel better. Diet and lifestyle may play a role in the prevention and treatment of many common illnesses and chronic diseases, such as Alzheimer's, Parkinson's, multiple sclerosis, diabetes, osteoporosis, heart disease, and lupus.

Even if we don't feel unwell today, our bodies can be under attack from our own lifestyle without our knowing it. If the connection between health and food or environment is an area of interest to you, I highly recommend you research for yourself. A good functional medical practitioner can be a tremendous support in this journey. Connections you discover and changes you make in your own home could change the trajectory of your family's life.

I was astonished to find that by simply altering Luke's diet, we saw results as different as night is from day. It was truly remarkable. He was a completely different kid when we carefully monitored his diet.

It's not rocket science to find ways to eat better or kick out the toxins, but it's a lifelong battle. We have to stay diligent. We might feel as if we have it all figured out one year, and then the next year we're under attack again. Awareness changes everything.

Remember that product ingredients and farming practices change over time. Just because our grandparents ate whole wheat bread for health doesn't mean it will not cause our body harm today. We need to stay on guard and always be learning. Our bodies change and may react differently than they did in the past. We need to stay aware of what is in our home and how we feel. An ever-evolving mix of toxins or change in our environment, or our own weakened immune system, can play a role in our health as well.

As our little guy began going to a church preschool, we realized he fell apart emotionally after eating the typical snacks provided to the kids. I was so diligent at home, but now I had to pay attention to what he ate at school.

Fruit snacks, cheddar fish crackers, and anything that contained dairy, sugar, soy, synthetic preservatives, or artificial coloring all became off limits. At the time I had never heard of gluten sensitivity, but today it would also be on my list of potential offenders.

Luke is an adult now (cue a few more mama tears), but I have continued to point him in the direction of staying aware of the food-health-emotion connection throughout his life. Of course, as he became a teen, his diet became even harder for me to control. But because I vowed to never let him forget what an impact diet can make, at age 14 he decided on his own to ditch the soda, candy, and chips often a part of a standard teen diet in favor of healthier choices.

One decision to kick out garbage and toxins in our diet and home today can have an impact on generations!

THE PROCESS OF CHANGE

Well-being involves winning the battle of the mind. Any choices we have to make aren't nearly as difficult when we've already made the decision to treat ourselves well so we can *be* well.

Sometimes our inner thoughts can become lazy and jeopardize our well-being. We feel deprived if we say no to fries and guilty if we give in. We feel great if we say yes to the gym but then defeated when we don't go the next day. We deem ice cream a reward and salad a punishment.

We don't have to do everything perfectly, but we need to be at peace with our choices.

We have to get our minds in the game, so we can call the shots on how we want to feel and what we do for our well-being. When we feel inspired and empowered by what a wellness lifestyle represents, we start to make positive choices more often. But we've grown accustomed to wanting the magic pill. The quick fix. Making better choices for our well-being doesn't begin by suddenly saying no to pancakes.

By continuing to eliminate or at least pare down what I don't need or have decided doesn't settle well with me, I start to feel more in control of my own well-being.

Even though my mind always tries to outsmart me, I've come up with a few tricks that work for me to keep my head in the game. Perhaps they'll work for you too.

Do you ever feel as if you can't say no to something you feel you deserve? Or you struggle to quit something that brings you comfort on some level?

Even when we know better, sometimes we just don't *feel* like making a change. Change is hard, especially when we've made being "unwell" our default for so long. It's hard to make the leap into a different pattern. Just like when we're on a merry-go-round already spinning at full speed, it feels scary to just jump off.

While sometimes we do need to give ourselves a little shove to take that first flying leap, we don't always have to do it that way. Sometimes we can just dangle our toes over the edge to slow the whirl a bit.

Whether it's a quest to find more joy, clear out toxins, kick an addiction, or start an exercise program, we can always do *something* simple to give us forward motion toward well-being.

You don't have to take a flying leap right now if you're not ready. And if you aren't paying attention, you might take a flying leap in the wrong direction, so first things first. We need to look at where we are and where we're going—baby steps.

Understanding that *change is a process* has helped me make more progress in so many areas of life. Greater wellness doesn't happen by chance luck or harnessing your own willpower to make one immediate change. It's about understanding where you are in the process, so you can create positive motion and develop habits that will become a productive part of your life.

5 STAGES OF CHANGE

1. *Precontemplation.* This stage is where an individual has not yet realized that their choices or their lifestyle is affecting them in a negative way.

2. *Contemplation.* This stage is where learning begins to take place. A person will consider the possibility that their choices are affecting their health. They're still ambivalent, but willing to look into it. Their old ways may still be enjoyable, but they may also experience some adverse consequences in their personal or family life, physical or psychological health, or well-being.

3. *Determination.* Individuals are ready to make serious changes for their health and wellness. They're convinced the effort will improve their well-being and believe the cons of continuing their old ways outweigh the pros.

4. *Action.* This is the stage where a plan is put into action and positive results begin to be seen! People keep pressing on until habits are a lifestyle.

5. *Maintenance.* A lifestyle comes from habits practiced over time. You might know that your body or emotions respond best to a certain diet, for example, but in this stage of change, if you grab a donut, you know how to get back on track. Once you've practiced your new habits and lifestyle choices for about six months, your old habits aren't as likely to pose a significant threat.

Discovering where I am or where I'm stuck in an area gives me clarity on what needs to come next. I may need to work on gathering more information, so I can get off the fence or develop certain habits and strategies or commit to a six-month maintenance plan.

I can be in several of these stages, depending on the changes I'm working on.

Examples

With water: I drink water every day, all day. I've mastered it. I'm in maintenance mode and have been for years. If I grabbed a soda instead, as tasty as it might sound, I'd immediately regret it and get back on track.

With housekeeping: I'm also in maintenance mode. Even though my house still becomes messy and cluttered for a period of time, I won't let it stay that way for long because how to fix it is ingrained in me now. I'm happier when the house is tidy.

With food choices: I'm solidly in action mode and have crossed over to maintenance mode in many ways.

With exercise: I've vacillated between determination mode and action mode my entire life (don't laugh). I think it's time to come up with a plan of action and set goals, so I can get to maintenance mode.

 Dwell Well: Think through your own successes and stages of well-being. How can you move forward in areas where you're stuck? Write out the stages of change in your journal. Leave room to identify areas you're working on and notes on your intentions and successes. Include dates so you can better keep track of progress.

streamlining
self-care

- Go on an automating spree. Put your bills on an auto-pay system. Sign up for an auto-shipment of some usual purchases (think groceries, household products, personal care products). Every little thing you automate will save you precious time and brain space!

- Think about one task you always do yourself that someone else could do instead. Sometimes we think we need to do it all ourselves, yet delegating can be a huge relief!

- When was the last time you set aside time to do something just for you? Open your calendar and pencil in a self-care date. Do something you've always wished you had time for. Sign up for a pottery class. Take dance lessons. Learn how to play tennis. Wander around a bookstore. Meet a life-giving friend for dessert. Learn a new language. Make it happen even if it means shuffling your commitments or cutting out something else in your busy schedule.

foraging

Gather Peace and Health from Nature

Foraging: To seek, gather, or hunt for plant matter.

Where flowers bloom, so does hope.
LADY BIRD JOHNSON

When I was little, the towering evergreens of Tryon Creek State Park behind my childhood home in Oregon became my playground. While neighborhood parents still deny the extent of our perceived unsupervised playtime, we felt safe and at peace, untethered and free to roam the forest to our heart's content.

Our little gang of friends loved to play *Little House on the Prairie* down by the creek, where imagination and ingenuity could turn fallen trees into covered wagons, log cabins, and whimsical beds and chairs. We'd gather leaves and bark, foraging for our "food" and wild provisions.

The forest left a lasting impression on me. When I close my eyes, I still remember that long walk down the pine needle–covered path that connected our backyard to the forest. The pure, complex scents wafting in the air, the feeling of pine needles crunching below my feet, the sounds of bubbling water and wind rustling through the trees awakened every sense.

Whether it was playing in a forest, sailing with my family on Puget Sound, or walking on the beach, spending time in nature as a kid engaged all of my senses, shaping for me what it feels like to be fully relaxed and present in my surroundings.

I think that I cannot preserve my health and spirits, unless
I spend four hours a day at least—and it is commonly more
than that—sauntering through the woods and over the hills
and fields, absolutely free from all worldly engagements.
HENRY DAVID THOREAU

These days a lot of us spend a significant amount of our lives indoors. Sadly, kids and adults alike are surrounded by more electronics than trees. The frantic pace and so-called conveniences of our modern life are conflicting with and diminishing our health and quality of life. Technology is at odds with the transformative power of nature.

Enjoying time in nature is a simple thing you can do for your well-being and self-care.

Taking a restorative walk is not only good for your physical health, but also for your mental health. While leaving behind the pace and stress in daily life is certainly a beneficial part of the experience, there's science behind the healing properties in nature. For example, forest therapy or forest bathing, which is spending time in a natural environment where all your senses are engaged. The practice is said to promote greater health, wellness, and happiness.

Essential oils secreted by trees are thought to have beneficial attributes for our health. Even a short daily trip into nature can boost mood, health, and well-being.[1]

These days my family feels fortunate to live right by another beautiful forested park, so we can take a nature walk whenever possible. Our dogs love it, and we always return home from our jaunt feeling a little lighter, happier, and more refreshed.

The good news is you don't have to live near a forest to introduce more nature into your daily life.

- Take a walk on a tree-lined street.

- Take kids on a nature treasure hunt, using the time to learn about plants.

- Visit a local garden, zoo, or nature preserve on the weekend.

- Bring plants and organic elements into your home.

- Plant a vegetable or flower garden.

- Wander through a park without an agenda.

- Study foraging (searching for wild food resources), and then give it a try.

- Go berry picking.

Take time away from home to be disconnected from devices and look for opportunities to be more mindful of natural elements around you. Take note of the beauty of trees, plants, and flowers. Breathe in the natural scents and notice your stress levels go down.

You might find that sights and sounds of nature can have a calming effect on you even by suggestion. Art depicting nature scenes for our home and apps or playlists of sounds from the forest or ocean, or of birds chirping, rain falling, or waterfalls may feel soothing and lower stress levels. Perhaps create your own nature view where there isn't one. Framed images of the sea or flower gardens, or a mural on the wall could inspire you.

In a world with so many distractions, sometimes a return to nature is just what the soul needs!

 Dwell Well: How do you feel when you're in nature? Is the experience rejuvenating? Write "Forest Therapy" as a heading in your journal. Jot down places you can go to observe nature and how you feel when you're more connected to nature.

BE A PLANT LADY

Even homebodies can experience some of the wonderful benefits of nature by being surrounded by organic elements in our own habitat. But…are you intimidated by plants? I hate to admit this, but I used to be known as a serial plant killer.

Phil and I were together for maybe six months before it appeared I was about to lose him. I just didn't have a clue how to take care of him. I really thought I could keep him alive; he had been such a healthy specimen right from the start. But it wasn't long before it became evident that Phil's days were numbered.

I had bought Phil to grace an empty corner in our home. We were on a photo deadline for my blog and the fiddle-leaf fig tree in the family room was no longer looking photogenic. Nothing like a beautiful green plant to bring a room to life, I always say. But a plant with brown shriveling leaves just wasn't going to beautifully illustrate the point.

Phil looked great for months, but sadly and predictably, it didn't take long for those healthy, deep green leaves to start turning a crunchy shade of brown. It was sad to watch, but one by one the leaves fell off until all that remained was another leafless stick in a pot.

I truly felt terrible about his condition, but I didn't know what else to do. He was an unrecognizable shadow of his former self. At the start of the summer, I'm ashamed to say, I set Phil outside in the far back corner of our backyard. By August I had pretty much forgotten about him. (So sorry, Phil.)

Unbeknownst to me, though, my husband had quietly started watering Phil and even turned him around now and then so he could get sunlight on all sides. One day I happened to look in that corner of the backyard and, much to my surprise, I spied a growing fiddle leaf! Happy joy. *Phil was alive!*

Since that day, I've turned over a new leaf, so to speak. I now think of myself as a plant lady. My plants not only have names, but I talk to them and I take care of them. In return, plants are therapeutic for me!

Houseplants not only bring a spa-like experience to a room, but many plants help to purify the indoor air quality too. And caring for living plants is relaxing!

Are you not sure what plants would be best for you? Visit a local garden center or nursery to ask what type of plant would thrive in your home.

If you're already a "crazy plant lady," and you were looking for permission to add a few extra plants to your home, there you go! Do it because it's good for your health.

Plants to try bringing into your home:

- aloe
- snake plant
- jade
- philodendron
- spider plant
- cast-iron plant
- spotted evergreen
- Devil's Ivy

As you decorate your home, plants and other organic textures such as flowers, wood pieces, botanicals, or other natural accessories can also create a sense of serenity and connection to nature.

If you look the right way, you can see
that the whole world is a garden.
FRANCES HODGSON BURNETT

A SECRET GARDEN

Years ago I lived in a 1920s home that had an established flower garden. It delighted me so much to cut my own roses and other blooms and foliage for my home each year. I often imagined the happiness those newly planted flowers likely brought to whoever originally tended to them. She (or he) might not have considered how grateful the future owners of the house would be, but the flower garden certainly brought me a lot of joy.

When we moved into our next home, a sweet little English cottage in Portland, the tiny backyard was mostly uninspiring. It consisted primarily of dirt, scraggly grass, and a concrete walkway. However, a beautiful maple tree stood at one corner, and a charming picket fence surrounded the perimeter.

While to this day I still don't consider myself an accomplished gardener, my lack of expertise hasn't lessened the benefits I've received from gardening. I discovered I not only enjoyed cutting flowers for the inside of my home, but that time spent designing and caring for a garden was therapeutic. As much as I love interiors, there was something invigorating, relaxing, and healing about working with my hands in the dirt and creating beauty with natural elements.

One summer I created an English-style garden in our backyard with fragrant creeping ground covers, rows of boxwoods, a sweet little bridge over a rock river bed, and stone pathways that twisted and curved throughout the garden. Through many seasons of life, our small garden was our sanctuary. It's where I felt closest to God, planting flowers in barren ground after heartbreaking loss. In happy times it was a place where our family could gather to celebrate the simple joys and milestones in life.

If you have even a small plot of land, you could create your own retreat from the world. Stress could melt away as you rest in a hammock hung between two trees or on a stand. A small table and chairs tucked into a corner of your yard or patio could be your destination for quiet reading or journaling.

When we moved into a new house, our backyard was nothing but sand. No trees, no fence, no flowers. I couldn't wait to claim one small corner of the yard for a secret garden that would stir my senses and bring rest to my soul.

We dug out space for a winding pea gravel pathway lined with rock edging, planted fragrant shrubs and flowers, put plants in pretty pots, set up trellises and metal arbors, and hung lanterns and twinkle lights.

I enjoyed taking my morning coffee to my secret garden to sit in the quiet. I would breathe in the fresh scent of the plants and flowers, letting the chaos of the world pause a little bit.

Time spent in a garden or creating one can restore a sense of balance within, helping you bloom where you are planted too.

> *Flowers always make people better, happier, and more*
> *helpful; they are sunshine, food and medicine for the soul.*
> **LUTHER BURBANK**

DESIGN YOUR OWN
SECRET FLOWER GARDEN

Flowers make people happier. If you've ever dreamed about having your own secret flower garden, make this the season to create one! Here are five steps:

1. *Pick a designated corner.* You don't need a lot of space for a secret garden. To create a magical backyard, a smaller space is even better. If your yard is huge, select a corner that could become your secret space. A back corner of a yard or a space tucked on a side of a house is often the best spot.

2. *Set up boundaries with screens and plants.* To have a truly secret space, you'll set up visual boundaries with screens and plants. A secret garden

should feel like a mystery that unfolds as you discover it. If you don't have mature plants or fences to surround it, you can begin with smaller border plants that help define your unique garden space. Be sure to add the aroma and beauty of romantic flowers! Tuck in a few vines on trellises for extra height.

3. *Add a gate or a door.* The best secret gardens have a magical entry. Add stepping stones and a gate or door at the entrance to make the space feel truly special and set apart. You can often find old gates or doors at secondhand stores, or you can create the illusion of one with an arbor or the placement of plants on either side of the walkway.

4. *Set up a garden table and chairs.* You'll want a spot to linger and dream. An old bench or café table and chairs can be the perfect invitation to stay awhile. If you have room, how about adding a hammock or a garden swing? Imagine a nap in a secret garden!

5. *Add twinkle lights and torches.* Create a magical mood with nighttime ambience. Add light to your garden with outdoor string lights. Lanterns can even have battery-operated candles for safety. Fire torches also can add warmth and beauty when you're enjoying your space in the evenings.

Once you've created your secret garden, it's up to you how you use it! Host friends for a secret garden book club or tea party. Invite a neighbor for a cup of coffee. Or keep the secret garden all to yourself. Putter around with your plants and flowers for relaxation. Bring out a sketch pad, notebook, or music for reflection.

Dwell Well: Write down your plan for your own secret garden and commit to starting it in the next week. In your journal, describe what it feels like to claim a space for yourself. How might this one act nourish you?

MAKE A MINIATURE GARDEN

If you don't have a large space for your secret garden, you can make a delightful, miniature-sized version for a patio table or countertop.

One summer I was inspired to make a miniature fairy garden in a wooden crate, complete with plants, tiny fencing, and furniture. My kids thought that was something an eccentric old lady would do, but you know what? I had fun. I shared it on my blog on a whim, and much to my surprise, my little fairy garden was eventually featured in publications all over the world. I guess I'm not alone in my eccentric hobbies.

You may also find joy in creating little gardens in a glass vessel or terrarium. Don't worry about whether you can keep a small plant alive in your small garden. The worst-case scenario is that you'll have to buy a five-dollar replacement. I'd say that's cheap therapy, wouldn't you?

13 WAYS GARDENING CAN INSPIRE SELF-CARE

1. Gardening inspires you to be more nurturing to yourself and others.

2. Gardening can be a peaceful (and healthy!) escape from the drama of the world. You can run from troubles in plenty of unhealthy ways. Use gardening as your escape instead.

3. Gardening can remind you to stop and smell the roses   literally.

4. Gardening is said to be helpful for relief from stress and trauma, so use it as a place of healing.

5. Growing a garden can help you feel more connected to your health.

6. Creating beauty in a garden inspires a positive mind-set.

7. A garden offers gratification of a job well done. Life can be challenging. As you put effort into your garden, you will see a return on investment and feel pride in what you helped to cultivate.

8. Gardening is a visual reminder to embrace seasons of growth. Spring always follows winter, providing something hopeful to look forward to in darker seasons.

9. Gardening is a great lesson in patience, a reminder that a little bit of effort every day (planting small seeds everywhere you go) adds up to big results!

10. Gardening teaches us to deal with what's overgrown in life and to weed out what's not bringing us joy.

11. Gardening can provide you with bouquets in every season and multiplies the joy of plants and flowers inside and out.

12. Gardening offers you alone time to recharge, but also an opportunity to connect with someone else. Invite your kids, spouse, or neighbors to visit your garden. Everyone feels more relaxed and open to conversation in a garden.

13. Gardening gives you time to collect your thoughts or work through something in your life, and even a clear enough head to find a solution!

BE THE GATEKEEPER

It's empowering to know how to create a healthy habitat for our families, one that can nurture and protect everything that matters to us. We are the gatekeepers of our home, responsible for what comes in. A home shelters the people we love, so of course we want to design a safe refuge from the world.

The more we adopt an organic approach to how we live and create a home, the better we all feel. Connecting with what is most natural is how we were designed to function best. If we apply that mind-set to everything in our surroundings, we'll be healthier for it.

Plants, furnishings, and colors can lift our spirits and inspire our well-being, but they can do only so much if the toxins in our products compromise everything we hold dear.

To feel our very best, we need to look at designing our home and life through a new lens. What does a healthy home look like? What does it smell like? What is truly clean? What are we putting into our body and on our skin?

The sad truth is many of the ingredients in personal care, cleaning, and beauty products are *not* pretty or good for us.

What we bring into our home matters.

Our personal care and cosmetic products may contain toxins such as lead, bismuth, parabens, and endocrine-disrupting phthalates, carcinogens, and other reproductive toxins. The soaps, body washes, deodorants, lotions, and cosmetics we lather on our skin, which is our largest organ, bring these toxicities into our body.

Because my husband and I see ourselves as the "gatekeepers" of our home, we're both eager to do whatever we can to make sure what enters our home is as safe as possible to keep our family healthy.

Like most parents, we tried to be diligent to protect our kids from what we thought might harm them. We locked our doors to be safer inside. We taught them to look both ways and held their hands when we crossed the street. We made them wear helmets on their bikes and seat belts in our cars. We taught them to eat their vegetables. We monitored their screen time and made them get fresh air and exercise.

We didn't get it all right, but we were willing to adapt when we learned new information or became aware of a healthier alternative. Because we knew common symptoms and conditions, anxieties, irritated skin, and haywire hormones could be clues that something wasn't right in our environment, we grew increasingly motivated to learn how to clean up our home and diet.

Just as we had scoured food ingredient lists when my son was a baby to protect him and continued to monitor anything that would trigger a reaction in him as he grew older, I knew it was worth it to eliminate unnecessary ingredients in and stress on our bodies in any way I could.

As I started to dig in further to research toxic ingredients and compare them to cleaning and personal care products under our sinks and in our cabinets, I discovered that even products *I invited into my home because I thought they were helping our family* (or at least just smelled good) may have posed unnecessary harm. Products I just assumed were *safe* contained toxins, known carcinogens, endocrine and reproductive disruptors, allergens, and more.

That was a hard discovery. I won't lie. No one likes to discover something they wish they would have been more diligent about years ago. Nevertheless, I've always found awareness and truth to be empowering. When we know better, we can do better going forward.

We can't necessarily control or even know everything that may negatively affect our environment, of course, and I'm aware I could do more. But I choose to not feel burdened by everything I'm not doing right now. Panicking, feeling paralyzed, or trying to sweep the potential concerns under the rug for sure don't help. I focus on educating myself and doing what I can.

As the gatekeepers, we have the freedom to be cautious about what comes into our dwelling and diligent about what needs to go. Just like the tile we choose or the style of our cabinets matter to us, *everything* we select for our home matters. Contrary to a wellness lifestyle being a burden or unnecessarily complicated, I find simplifying our choices to be freeing.

- I no longer stroll the aisles at the grocery store trying to decide what cleaning products to use (while holding my breath because the scents overwhelmed me as soon as I got to the aisle). I don't need all that stuff!

- I no longer worry about passing out or wearing a gas mask to clean my bathroom.

- I no longer wonder about the safety of products I have under our sink, in our cabinets, or on our bodies.

- I don't buy junk that causes my skin to itch or break out in a rash.

- I enjoy making our home smell lovely naturally because I know the plants and essential oils I bring in are helping, not harming, our bodies.

- I focus more on self-care and preventative wellness, and as a result I'm no longer exhausted from toxic overload the way I used to be.

- My mind is clear and more focused than it's ever been.

- I feel better knowing I've done all I know to do to protect our home.

 Dwell Well: How are you already a gatekeeper? Write down three statements about what you're doing that is healthy. Next, list three goals you have as a gatekeeper.

DETOX YOUR CLEANING ROUTINE

Whether a chemical poses a real and known danger to your health, or even a less likely one, why risk having an abundance of potentially toxic ingredients in your home when you don't have to? That's my perspective. Many nontoxic alternatives are available, so as far as I'm concerned more natural ingredients yield the best results when it comes to our well-being.

If we don't need to be lathering potentially harmful chemicals on our bodies, breathing them in our air, or using them to clean our dishes, counters, clothing, or home, why not use something less taxing on them?

Do I still have questionable or unstudied products in my house? Of course! But we are working our way through our home, evaluating what is beneficial and working on making more organic and natural choices going forward.

Unfortunately, even a product labeled as plant based, organic, natural, or derived from essential oils won't necessarily ensure it's entirely safe. Any product can be labeled natural and even have some plant-based ingredients in it and yet contain harmful fillers or preservatives.

Ideally, purchase household products from a company you trust, one that has a clear commitment to quality ingredients.

Yes, it can take a bit of research to determine what and whom to trust, but I find any effort is worth it for the confidence our family has in bringing products into our home and trusting the company we are purchasing from.

Every little positive step we take helps lessen the stress on our bodies and promotes greater well-being in our homes, setting a good trajectory toward our overall health.

NONTOXIC CLEANERS/DIY ALTERNATIVES

The more we know, the better we can do. Cleaning doesn't need to be more difficult than necessary. Buying less junk to begin with and using plant-based ingredients makes the whole experience more pleasant.

It's so easy and economical to make your own products! What could be easier than cleaning with baking soda and vinegar? You can even jazz up the scent with a drop of your favorite essential oil.

DIY NONTOXIC CLEANING WITH BAKING SODA

- Clean your sink with the leftover half of a lemon or a slice of lemon and a sprinkle of baking soda.

- Sprinkle your sink with baking soda and scrub with warm water and a wet rag.

- Clean your sink drain by pouring ½ cup of baking soda down the drain, and then ½ cup vinegar. After it fizzes, pour 6 cups hot water down the drain.

- Make a toilet bowl cleaner with ¼ cup baking soda and 1 cup vinegar.

- Make an all-purpose cleaner with ½ cup vinegar, ¼ cup baking soda, and ½ gallon water.

ALL THE ESSENTIALS

If you're ready to start ditching synthetic chemicals and toxins and are intrigued by the healing power of plants, you might be curious to learn more about the benefits of essential oils. Incorporating essential oils into our home and daily routine began to change how my family lives and feels in truly amazing ways.

As I've become more mindful of the ingredients in everything we purchase and consume, I've also turned to essential oils to support wellness daily. I'm not only a homebody and a plant lady, but I can add "crazy oil lady" to my résumé too.

What are essential oils and what do they do? Essential oils are highly concentrated and volatile liquids (meaning they evaporate easily into the air) extracted from trees, shrubs, flowers, stems, and seeds. They are the most powerful part of the plant, and the oils serve to naturally defend plants from disease, insects, and harsh weather conditions. They are necessary for a plant to grow, live, evolve, and adapt to its surroundings.

When you "stop and smell the roses," besides slowing down, you receive a health- and mood-boosting benefit from the plant itself.

Essential oils benefit us humans too. Millions of people around the world have used them safely and effectively for health and beauty for thousands of years. Historically, they are the oldest known form of medicine, dating back to 4500 BC. Essential oils contain the most powerful plant compounds found in nature. They're so effective that they're still used as an active ingredient in many common prescription and over-the-counter drugs.

You may steer clear of them, thinking of oils as strange little potions used by only the crunchiest of hippies. Yet they are not something to be afraid of. Whether or not you realize it, you have received the positive effects of essential oils in your environment your entire life. Essential oils are often used to flavor common food and beverages, as well as to scent many products. Every time you wandered in a forest, you experienced their transforming power.

Today, many health-conscious consumers are discovering the benefits of using these plant-based extracts for everything from homeopathic remedies to skincare, beauty regimens, and toxin-free cleaning. There is growing scientific research that offers proof of their powerful benefits too.[2]

It's important to note that essential oils are *not* the same thing as fragrance (or parfum/perfume). Fragrance is listed as an ingredient in many personal care products and may contain ingredients that could be harmful to us.

Also noteworthy is that just because a bottle or household product is labeled as containing pure essential oils doesn't mean it's good for you. The product may be compromised in quality or tainted with fillers, preservatives, and perfumes. It's important to do research on ingredients of any products you use, as well as the standards and practices of the company itself to ensure you're receiving the highest quality and benefits of essential oils.

It's not difficult to begin to incorporate essential oils into your home. One of the easiest ways to start is to put essential oils with water into a diffuser. Ultrasonic diffusers combine the advantages of an air purifier, humidifier, atomizer, and aromatherapy diffuser into one by breaking a mixture of essential oils and water into millions of microparticles and dispersing them invisibly into the air.

Don't worry if the scent of the oils isn't at first what you expected. Plants don't smell like their synthetic imposters (gratefully). If you don't immediately love the smell (although many essential oils will be love at first sniff), your nose and body will eventually thank you. I promise that before you know it, you'll crave the scent and benefits of essential oils and cringe when you catch a whiff of the synthetic scents you used to love.

Who doesn't feel better and breathe more deeply when the rains have refreshed the air and cleansed the environment? That's how it feels to inhale these pure plant oils!

- Put a drop of your favorite essential oil on your wrist as a perfume and mood-booster.

- Add a drop of lemon essential oil to your DIY household cleaner recipe.

- Mix lavender, tea tree oil, or copaiba into your haircare or skincare products and moisturizer.

- Make an essential oil linen spray to refresh your sheets.

- Ditch toxic room sprays and create your own lovely signature home scents.

Not only is creating your own diffuser blends with oils and making DIY essential oil products a relaxing and enjoyable activity; but inhaling certain pure essential oils can often change how we feel immediately.

Essential oils positively affect our health and well-being in many ways. Inhaling the aroma of essential oils triggers parts of our brains that govern memories, emotions, learning, and behavior. Certain oils can naturally improve our moods, sparking joy and making us feel calm, energized, or inspired. We can even use essential oils to create positive associations. For instance, if your beloved aunt had a lavender bush, you probably already have a pleasant association with lavender. Our emotions, memories, and scents are intricately connected!

It's important to go slow when introducing new oils to your nose or body because they're so powerful. Essential oils can be used to build up our body's natural defenses, so we can fight back when needed and stay above the wellness line as much as possible. They enhance our well-being as well as make the atmosphere of our home healthier and cleaner. Essential oils may promote better mental focus and happier hormones, improve mood, support healthy immune systems, provide natural options for prettier skin, and offer a more relaxed and restful sleep.

DIFFUSER RECIPES

Wake Up

4 drops peppermint

4 drops lemon

Breathe Easy

3 drops eucalyptus

3 drops peppermint

Carefree

4 drops orange

3 drops bergamot

2 drops ylang-ylang

Sleep Tight

3 drops cedarwood

2 drops lavender

foraging
self-care

- Breathe in plant goodness. Put a drop of an essential oil in your hand (try bergamot or eucalyptus), cup it over your nose, and take a few slow, deep breaths. Plants can help you relax, calm down, re-center, start the day off right, and boost your mood.

- Go for a wander. Head out on a walk with no end destination in mind. Roam around and enjoy nature. Forage. Be mindful of how you feel and what you see. Come home refreshed.

- Plant a succulent in a teacup or herbs in a pot for your kitchen windowsill.

nourishing

Feed Your Mind, Body, and Spirit

Nourish: 1. to sustain with food or nutriment;
supply with what is necessary for life, health, and growth;
2. to cherish, foster, keep alive, etc.
3. to strengthen, build up, or promote.

---

*The best things are nearest: breath in your nostrils, light in
your eyes, flowers at your feet, duties at your hand, the path
of God just before you. Then do not grasp at the stars, but
do life's plain, common work as it comes, certain that daily
duties and daily bread are the sweetest things in life.*

ROBERT LOUIS STEVENSON

Nothing is quite like the knot that forms in your stomach as you're emptying your vacation fund to repair the most unglamorous hidden corners of your home. A broken sewer, electrical system, or water heater can throw a serious wrench (see what I did there?) in the joy of homebody life.

Like many homeowners, I've had to deal with my fair share of spendy repairs and preventative maintenance. Despite all of the hard work and love we pour into our dwelling, even a home built on a strong foundation may not be enough to weather every storm.

My own family has had to leave the comforts of our nest and even move away from homes we loved many times. Emotional stress and strain grew right under the shelter of our own roof. Financial pressures threatened to shut off our personal comforts and even steal the joy of what we dreamed would be a "forever home."

Our family has gone through scary times in the supposed safety of our home. We've faced medical crises, mourned losses, and even watched helplessly as flood-waters from a raging river lapped right at the front door of my parents' home, threatening to wash it away in a surge of waves.

Hurt, pain, or suffering isn't always fixed by simply returning to the safety of home. Of that, I am sure. In some seasons of life we don't even have a home to return to, so a structure cannot be our anchor.

To feel strong and able, we need more than just cozy shelter for safety. We need to nourish *ourselves*, the essence of who we are. This will be the body we live in, the dwelling that holds the mind we rely on and the spirit we carry with us, so proper care and feeding is essential.

We want healthy kids, strong marriages, and good relationships, and we all know we can benefit from nourishing ourselves. Yet does any woman among us take *perfect* care of herself at all times? If so, I don't believe I've met her. We care for kids, keep up with jobs, run errands, prepare meals, clean the house, and do the grocery shopping while maybe finding time to brush our hair occasionally. We can add any number of unique stressors and responsibilities to our individual to-do lists, and it's no wonder most of us struggle to find time or energy for ourselves.

Does anyone do it all?

Even if a woman tries to do it all well with all her might, she understandably begins to feel overextended, out of balance, or stressed out. We all suffer the results of living in a sped-up, overstuffed, overscheduled life. Making time to nourish yourself may feel like another exhausting-sounding expectation on an already over-flowing to-do list—especially if you're a go-getter, pedal-to-the-metal, keep-every-one-else-happy kind of gal!

Who feels they have time to pamper themselves when there are jobs to do, humanitarian causes to fight for, and other people to take care of? You have important things on your to-do list. I get that. I do too.

But protecting and caring for our own mind, body, and spirit first is the most beneficial thing we can do for ourselves, as well as for the people we care about.

Have you seen this funny quote around the internet or on a sign somewhere?

First I drink the coffee. Then I do the things.

For our well-being journey, perhaps we should make a slight revision:

First I breathe. Then I do the things.

The health benefits of drinking coffee can be debatable, but the benefits of breathing are a given.

If you're like many women, you're probably charging ahead to do the things while expecting breathing will somehow happen naturally. It's nice to be able to cross one effortless thing off our list. Am I right?

Breathe √

We breathe in, we breathe out. Oxygen fills our lungs and is spread to every part of our body. It's a healthy, automated rhythm that breathes life in us, so we can thrive in all of the ways we were designed to thrive. When we can breathe, we can feel joy, fulfill our purpose, and function at our best.

Isn't that a picture of what we all long for?

We want to fill ourselves with the good stuff. The things that will nourish us. Things that bring us to life!

You weren't meant to run laps without oxygen. It's okay to exhale and take something off your plate. No one can keep up *without* breath in her lungs. If you've ever struggled to breathe for any reason, you immediately become aware that what seemed simple isn't as effortless as it was. If anything interrupts that natural rhythm of breath in, breath out…suddenly you can't do any of the things.

Likewise, we need to fill ourselves with what fuels us and find a rhythm of living that makes us feel more balanced, healthier, and stronger inside and out. If we're struggling to function in an ordinary day, barely finding time to take a breath, that's exactly what we need to do—stop and breathe in more of what we need to thrive.

you don't have to hold your breath and hold up the world.

When you're in doubt about what to do next on the to-do list, make sure you put on the oxygen mask first. As the saying goes, you cannot pour from an empty cup. Nor can you breathe without oxygen! Nourishing yourself in spirit, mind, and body fills you with the fuel you need to do all of the things you were created to do.

Then you can do the things.

GET AROUND TO IT

When I initially considered growing our own vegetables, the first thing I did was buy all of the backyard garden books I could find. I didn't want to accidentally make some fatal gardening mistake, so I thought I should have many resources and do as much research as I could before I got started.

My effort slowed me down. I'd bought so many books that I became overwhelmed by information. I didn't have time to read it all, let alone time to get out there and implement all the knowledge I would ever need to become a master gardener before I planted my first seed in the ground.

Likewise, you have to start somewhere with self-care, so find small ways you can jump in. The best time to start is always today.

Trying to be prepared for everything and know all of the things you'd ever need to know before you act on anything can be so inefficient and counterproductive.

Robert Fulghum wrote a poem and subsequent book about how everything we really need to know we learned in kindergarten. Well, I also learned a valuable life lesson on the first day of school in third grade.

My teacher handed all of the students a round circle cut from cardstock with the words *To It* printed in the middle. She wanted to make sure we could never say "I didn't get a round to it." Get it?

In a lightning-paced life full of responsibilities, it really is crazy hard to "find the time" to get around to taking care of *yourself* in a holistic way.

Taking any step at all does more for us than just thinking about it. Time for well-being isn't something you'll just happen to *find*, anyway. That approach is bound to be frustrating. You must intentionally nurture well-being.

In your journal, draw a circle and add "To It" inside it. Remind yourself that you already have what you need to take care of yourself. Not getting around to it is an excuse. You have everything you need, so let's start right now.

Dwell Well: Start a new page in your journal and title it "Daily Self-Care List." What will be your daily nonnegotiables when it comes to nourishing yourself? Start with simple things you know you can do immediately to build up your spirit, mind, and body.

Don't cover the entire page with future or unrealistic expectations. Give yourself grace, friend. If, as mine tends to do, your mind starts whirling with ideas, create a page for self-care practices and ideas you might use only on occasion. Fill in your thoughts as you keep reading and become inspired. Feel free to let ideas stir, soak in, and develop.

The most important step is to focus on being more mindful about the steps you will incorporate immediately.

SPIRIT

If you've ever hopped aboard an airplane in a storm, you've likely experienced that glorious moment when the plane finally ascends above the turmoil, through the dark layer of clouds, to reveal the brilliant sunshine and blue skies that were there all along.

Perspective changes everything, doesn't it?

Our culture often suggests that everything we need for fulfillment is gained through our own wisdom, possessions, experiences, and accomplishments. The Bible's book of Ecclesiastes teaches that genuine well-being cannot be found through our own wisdom, nor our pleasure, achievements, or belongings. If we tether our meaning in life to an ever-moving horizon, a true state of well-being and peace will always be elusive, just beyond our grasp. Ultimate well-being isn't found anywhere under the sun. Everything in the universe derives its meaning from God.

To gain a better perspective, we must rise above the clouds to see life from the vantage point of the spiritual realm. God intends for us to be free from what is temporal in this life, and to live for something bigger.

Nourish Your Soul

Brother Lawrence, a seventeenth-century monk, cultivated a lifelong practice of dwelling in the presence of God by acknowledging the Spirit in his life even as he went about mundane daily tasks.

His letters and conversations are recorded by his own hand and by his close friend Joseph de Beaufort, in a classic spiritual book called *The Practice of the Presence of God*.

"Brother Lawrence insisted that, to be constantly aware of God's presence, it is necessary to form the habit of continually talking with Him throughout each day. To think that we must abandon conversation with Him in order to deal with the world is erroneous. Instead, as we nourish our souls by seeing God in His exaltation, we will derive a great joy."[1]

I began to live as though there were no one but God and myself in the world…We cannot avoid the dangers of life without God's continual help, so we should ask Him for it ceaselessly. But how can we ask for help unless we are with Him? To be with Him, we must cultivate the holy habit of thinking of Him often…We have to know someone before we can truly love him. In order to know God, we must think about Him often. Once we get to know Him, we will think about Him even more often, because where our treasure is, there also is our heart![2]

Those who live according to the flesh have their
minds set on what the flesh desires; but those
who live in accordance with the Spirit have
their minds set on what the Spirit desires.

ROMANS 8:5

Scripture tells us if we acknowledge the Spirit's presence in our life, He will guide us and direct our path. The book of Romans explains that if we live according to the world's perspective, we do not have the Spirit of Christ in us.

You, however, are not in the realm of the flesh but
are in the realm of the Spirit, if indeed the Spirit
of God lives in you. And if anyone does not have
the Spirit of Christ, they do not belong to Christ.

ROMANS 8:9

Brother Lawrence describes how he cultivated a relationship with the Spirit even in the day-to-day moments of taking care of the monastery kitchen:

There is not in the world a kind of life more sweet and delightful than that of a continual conversation with God. Those only can comprehend it who practice and experience it…He does not ask much of us, merely a thought of Him from time to time, a little act of adoration, sometimes to pray for His grace, sometimes to offer Him your sufferings, and sometimes to return Him thanks for the favors He has given you, and still gives you, in the midst of your troubles, and to console yourself with Him the oftenest you can. Lift up your heart to Him, sometimes even at your meals, and when you are in company; the least little remembrance will always be acceptable to Him. One need not cry out very loud; He is nearer to us than we are aware of…[3]

Take courage…The difficulties of life do not have to be unbearable. It is the way we look at them—through faith or unbelief—that makes them seem so…God often allows us to go through difficulties to purify our souls and teach us to rely on Him more (1 Peter 1:6-7). So offer Him your problems unceasingly and ask Him for the strength to overcome them. Talk to Him often. Forget Him as seldom as possible. Praise Him. When the difficulties are at their worst, go to Him humbly and lovingly—as a child goes to a loving father—and ask for the help you need from His grace…We should be careful to never separate ourselves from His presence. We must dwell with Him always.[4]

How to Build a Strong Spiritual Foundation

No matter how wise or prepared we are, life doesn't always go according to our plans. In the moments when the weight of the world feels as if it's resting on our shoulders—when we're facing a serious or chronic illness, the loss of someone we love, a financial burden, or another momentous event or circumstance—we can become even more aware of our weakness in our spiritual perspective.

How can we build a stronger spiritual foundation for ourselves, our home, and our family, one that will nourish us and stand firm even through the storms of life? We can study and meditate on Scripture to fill our heart, soul, and mind with truth and promises.

meditating on scripture will reset your perspective on what is happening around you.

- Trust in the LORD with all your heart and lean not on your own understanding; in all your ways submit to him, and he will make your paths straight (Proverbs 3:5-6).

- These commandments that I give you today are to be on your hearts. Impress them on your children. Talk about them when you sit at home and when you walk along the road, when you lie down and when you get up. Tie them as symbols on your hands and bind them on your foreheads. Write them on the doorframes of your houses and on your gates (Deuteronomy 6:6-9).

- As for everyone who comes to me and hears my words and puts them into practice, I will show you what they are like. They are like a man building a house, who dug down deep and laid the foundation on rock. When a flood came, the torrent struck that house but could not shake it, because it was well built. But the one who hears my words and does not put them into practice is like a man who built a house on the ground without a foundation. The moment the torrent struck that house, it collapsed and its destruction was complete (Luke 6:47-49).

- Everyone who hears these words of mine and puts them into practice is like a wise man who built his house on the rock (Matthew 7:24).

SCRIPTURE MEDITATION
FOR WHEN YOU NEED COMFORT

Do you want to feel closer to God?

Come near to God and he will come near to you (James 4:8).

Do you feel emotionally distraught?

Trust in the LORD with all your heart and lean not on your own understanding; in all your ways submit to him, and he will make your paths straight (Proverbs 3:5-6).

Do you feel anxious or afraid?

Cast all your anxiety on him because he cares for you (1 Peter 5:7).

Are you worried about the future?

Do not worry about tomorrow, for tomorrow will worry about itself. Each day has enough trouble of its own (Matthew 6:34).

Are you heartbroken?

He heals the brokenhearted and binds up their wounds (Psalm 147:3).

Are you burdened by overwhelming situations in your life?

God is our refuge and strength, an ever-present help in trouble (Psalm 46:1).

Do you struggle with discontent or jealousy?

I am not saying this because I am in need, for I have learned to be content whatever the circumstances. I know what it is to be in need, and I know what it is to have plenty. I have learned the secret of being content in any and every situation, whether well fed or hungry, whether living in plenty or in want. I can do all this through him who gives me strength (Philippians 4:11-13).

Are you fearful?

Do not fear, for I am with you; do not be dismayed, for I am your God. I will strengthen you and help you; I will uphold you with my righteous right hand (Isaiah 41:10).

Are you suffering?

I consider that our present sufferings are not worth comparing with the glory that will be revealed in us (Romans 8:18).

Do you need to forgive?

Get rid of all bitterness, rage and anger, brawling and slander, along with every form of malice. Be kind and compassionate to one another, forgiving each other, just as in Christ God forgave you (Ephesians 4:31-32).

Do you feel purposeless?

"I know the plans I have for you," declares the LORD, "plans to prosper you and not to harm you, plans to give you hope and a future" (Jeremiah 29:11).

Are you weary?

From the ends of the earth I call to you, I call as my heart grows faint; lead me to the rock that is higher than I (Psalm 61:2).

- -

As you develop a strong spiritual mind-set, you keep your mind anchored above. No matter how distant from God or unworthy you might feel, you are worthy and invited into a relationship with Him.

"Peace I leave with you; my peace I give to you.
I do not give to you as the world gives. Do not let
your hearts be troubled and do not be afraid."

JOHN 14:27

MIND

The creator of the universe made you, so don't bring yourself down by doubt or critical self-talk, or by focusing on your less than ideal traits. Practice looking at who you are from a heavenly vantage point. Gauge your growth and the measure of what you accomplish from a spiritual perspective. As you do this, you will renew your mind and perspective.

A wise person is hungry for knowledge,
while the fool feeds on trash.
PROVERBS 15:14 NLT

Nourish Your Mind

When our kids were younger, my husband and I wanted to get out and walk in our neighborhood together every day. But once our schedule took over, we would head in different directions and never fit in that walk. We finally decided the only way walking was going to happen was to make it a priority every morning.

Our girls were old enough to be alone with their brother in the early hours of the morning, so we made a commitment to walk at the ungodly hour of 6:00 a.m. It sounded like a good idea—until the alarm went off. It was dark. And rainy. So we pushed the snooze button. And pushed it again.

It became clear that if we wanted to avoid procrastination, we had to eliminate the snooze button option. No snooze button. No debating about the weather. Rain or shine, we heard our alarm and got out of bed. To say we dreaded getting up and walking out the door at that hour in the rain would be an understatement. We loathed it. Yet once we started walking, we were rewarded with fresh air, exercise, and time together. Doing what we said we'd do took intentional effort, but it was worth it.

Mel Robbins, in her book *The 5 Second Rule*, says we make 35,000 decisions every day. She confirms what we experienced in our early morning walking days. The snooze button is not our friend. Mel points out that if the first decision of the day is to hit the snooze button, that small act conditions our mind to procrastinate throughout the day.

One of my life challenges has been to learn to take positive, measurable action on what I know I need to do. Like a computer with too many tabs open, my mind keeps all of the possibilities available and in front of me. Instead of focusing on the essentials, I'm all over the place.

I think many women relate to that feeling of being overwhelmed. Without clear focus and intention, it's difficult to do what we really want to do to properly care for ourselves. Our mind is a powerful tool given to us to help us take care of ourselves, to live life to the full, and fulfill our spiritual and earthly purpose. Harnessing its potential can help us accomplish the good we want to do (without feeling as if we're losing our mind in the process).

Yet as beneficial as leaping out of bed when the alarm goes off is, harnessing our mind's potential isn't always that simple. A mind that isn't cooperating is challenging. My husband dealt with depression for the first two-thirds of our marriage, and I had my own bouts of anxiety, so I know it's difficult when our inner thoughts aren't directing us as we want them to. Suffering through those times has given me greater compassion for others who go through similar difficulties and an opportunity to learn how to better nourish myself. I was going to sink or swim, so I figured out how to swim.

First and foremost, if you struggle with any illness at all, don't be ashamed or afraid to ask for help. I tend to be a self-sufficient gal and don't ask for much help in life, but medication in those seasons was a godsend. It helped my mind settle down enough that I was able to work on my inner thoughts, mind-sets, and habits. Asking for help can be a brave and powerful step in healing—not only for yourself, but also for those around you.

Disciplining myself to have more control of my inner thoughts over the years has brought me to a place where I have more peace of mind. I wouldn't say I'm 100 percent free of anxiety; I know my mind is still prone to run in that direction. But I feel stronger and better equipped to help myself ride through or rise above stress than ever before.

A focus on nourishing my mind and harnessing my inner thoughts has resulted in greater capacity to do what I feel called to do. Fueling my body with the healthy things it needs to thrive and eliminating both the physical and emotional toxic junk that used to fog my head has given me more strength and clarity to chase dreams and meet the needs of the people I care about.

MAKE HEALTHY CONNECTIONS

Surround yourself with positive people who not only encourage and understand you, but who challenge you to be better and motivate you to reach your goals. Talk to a counselor to work through difficulties. Journal your innermost thoughts. Listen to motivating podcasts and speakers who can keep your thoughts optimistic and focused on what you have to offer the world.

HELP YOUR AUTHENTIC SELF SHINE

Get to know your true self. I think one of the most stressful experiences is trying to be or even pretend to be someone we aren't. Give your mind the gift of being comfortable with who you are. Get better in tune with your own mind so you can recognize when and how to take action for yourself.

Do you need to recharge with friends or have time alone? Get to know when you need a break from *doing* so you can focus on collecting your thoughts.

Take a personality test to give yourself perspective. Are you an introvert, extrovert, or a combination? Personality tests can help you see your strengths and weaknesses. It's not about labeling yourself or feeling bad about who you are. Learning more about how you think will help you understand why you are the way you are and how you can best interact with others. When you understand who you are, you feel more empowered to let your authentic self shine!

Dwell Well: Who is the real you? Write for ten or more minutes about who you are at your core. What might surprise others? In what way or what area have you been pretending to be someone or something you're not? How good would it feel to move toward authenticity? Write about a way you might do this, even with baby steps!

Listen to Your Own Mind

These days it's tempting to scroll our time away, mindlessly checking out the creativity others contribute to the world. Rather than filling your mind with the frenzied pace of everyone else's thoughts, for a period every day turn off the devices, the TV, Netflix, and social media. Practice being present and listening to your own mind. If your brain races, read through your journal. Calm your mind with a soundtrack that helps to relax and focus your thoughts. Give yourself margins for quiet contemplation and time for creativity to flourish.

Be a Learner

A healthy mind is always learning. My husband loves to do jigsaw puzzles, study Scripture, and memorize the definitions of vocabulary words to keep his mind strong. My dad went back to school to get an advanced degree in his seventies, plays video games with my kids, and learns how to use every gadget under the sun just for fun.

Read a Book

Books can fill your mind with knowledge, inspiration, or new perspectives. Reading sharpens your mind and makes you more creative.

Learn a Hobby

Get inspired for a new hobby, challenging your mind to learn new skills. Even online you can learn how to play an instrument, get voice lessons, learn how to paint or knit, or acquire just about any new skill you've ever wanted to have—and often for free!

Learn a New Strategy

For professional or entrepreneurial ventures, expand your knowledge for your business. Read books or watch videos on strategy. Ask to meet with others who have experience. Find a mentor who can encourage you and hold you accountable.

Always be learning something new to move yourself and your dreams forward. Don't limit your potential. The mind is capable of learning new things when we commit ourselves to growing!

SIMPLIFY YOUR THOUGHT PROCESS

If your mind feels overwhelmed all the time, maybe you just need to simplify! You might be making certain tasks more complicated than they need to be. Change can be hard, but the effort to simplify can be freeing to your time and mind space.

Find ways to go through your daily tasks more efficiently. Which things could you "set and forget" so your mind doesn't have to rethink and take action every time?

For instance, if at work you often have to answer the same customer questions on email, write templates you can copy and paste later to save your brain from reinventing those wheels. I use the notes section in my phone to keep important information organized and easy to find. It's so handy for me to be able access details as needed.

Use a phone calendar to keep track of appointments and tasks so you don't have to worry about forgetting anything. You might feel more efficient when you can write things down but still carry them with you on the go.

HAVE THE COURAGE TO BE IMPERFECT

Trying to be perfect is exhausting. Don't beat yourself up if your progress on goals or a project is slow, or if you've taken a few steps back. Success isn't all or nothing; accepting imperfection makes big goals attainable. Baby steps will get you where you're going, even if the road isn't perfect.

LAUGH AT YOURSELF

Laughing at yourself is said to produce better resilience and greater well-being. Don't become too defensive. Your mistakes don't make you less worthy of love or acceptance. Own your weaknesses and use mistakes as a chance to grow. It's okay to not get everything right all the time. Have a sense of humor when mistakes happen, and don't bring down everyone around you. Keep your spirits up and do your part to make things right again. People who can laugh at themselves and not take everything so seriously are more fun to be around, and they give others permission to lighten up too.

Practice Positive Mind-Sets

Consistently add journaling to your morning or evening routine. Journaling can be an opportunity to get thoughts out of your mind and onto paper. Use it to move away from fear and forward in healthy ways. Write out your prayers. Write down positive action steps to sort out your hurt feelings rather than lashing out or gossiping to someone else. Refocus fears and problems into positives and possibilities. Use your journal to jot down what you're grateful for that day or dreams for the future. Fill it with positive thoughts, scriptures, motivating mind-sets, and encouraging words to inspire you. Flip back to the page with your lovely list often and review it.

Be Mindful

Don't just let things *happen* to you; practice being mindful of what *is* happening. Create the experiences you want in your life. Be present in moments that matter rather than letting your mind wander off, trying to keep up with everything at once. Think about what you're doing in your day and why you're doing it. Are your actions contributing to your well-being? Rather than letting anxious feelings escalate out of control, be more mindful of your thoughts. Harvard Business School Professor Alison Wood Brooks has conducted many studies to show that simply reframing *anxiety* as *excitement* helps you feel more in control.

Bring Joy to Mind

Find ways to daily bring joy to your mind as a deliberate choice.

Create a joy-filled playlist to listen to rather than filling your mind with the rants of others or bad news on social media.

Rather than creating a negative loop of fears or worries in your mind or reviewing lists of failures, hurts, wounds, or frustrations that bring you down, use your notebook to cultivate a list of the joy bringers. In your journal, title a page "Choose Joy." Fill it with thoughts or activities that bring a sense of joyfulness. Whenever you feel overwhelmed or stressed out, read through your joy list and treat yourself to healthy activities that refresh your mind, body, and spirit.

Dwell Well: How will you nourish your mind? From the ideas we just explored, choose two that feel like the right choices for you. Write down goals for these categories or your first thoughts about this commitment to yourself and your well-being.

BODY

"How are you today, friend?"

I always answer that question with "I'm fine." If I were to ask you how you're doing, I'm guessing you'd say you're fine too.

But if we stop everything and *think* about how we feel, the answer might be different.

We say we're fine because it's the expected answer. Who wants to be a Debbie Downer, anyway?

But I think we sometimes forget what it feels like to feel great. Or we're too busy to notice when we don't. Nearly a decade ago I had a wake-up call, reminding me that saying I'm fine and *being* fine are not the same.

I woke up one August morning with a pain in my abdomen that just wouldn't go away. I don't like to visit doctors, but this was one of those things you know must be checked sooner than later. I woke up my husband, and we drove to a local clinic. Apparently, it was my gallbladder acting up. Great! So inconvenient! I'd never had gallbladder trouble before.

Why now? I asked myself. We were in one of the most stressful and busiest seasons of our life, having just moved away from family and friends. We had two house payments for two homes in two different states, Jerry was trying to start a new church in a new-to-us community, we were all trying to make new friends, and our kids had enrolled in new schools. I was actively growing my business. But even though I ate healthy food and was convinced I was taking good care of myself, the stress I'd been trying to ignore was catching up with me.

I'm not a physician, so I won't attempt to explain how or why one's body parts might break down, but over time I've learned that my body is often good at alerting me when something is amiss or out of balance. I think it helps to become a student of our own body. Over the years I've had to start paying closer attention to how I feel, interpreting what my body needs and, of course, making healthy changes for my future self whether or not I think I need to.

After an ultrasound, I was told my gallbladder was "angry." The doctor looked at me funny and basically asked how I managed to not notice it was unhappy. *I'm not sure. I guess I was busy?* She explained that, basically, my gallbladder was rupturing, and all sorts of toxic junk would be flowing into my body if they didn't take care of it immediately.

That was awesome. I had somehow managed to keep everyone else happy and healthy but had angered my own gallbladder. A doctor handed me papers to sign and a nurse asked if I wanted some drugs. Unfortunately, my gallbladder was so far gone that this wasn't going to be one of those quick laparoscopic surgeries. I'd likely be sporting a four- or five-inch scar the rest of my life as a souvenir.

Watching tears spill from my daughter's eyes nearly broke my heart as the doctor explained how potentially risky my surgery was because of the condition of my gallbladder. Luckily, I was completely knocked out before I had a chance to panic or reprimand myself any further.

The next thing I knew, I was awake, and I immediately felt relieved. *Thank You, Lord, for letting me live!*

Nourish Your Body

I'd love to say that from that point on I've taken perfect care of myself, and that I always listen to my body and will never again be responsible for missing an important clue to my health or well-being. But while I can't say that, I am learning to do better. In fact, I feel better than ever, likely because of the accumulation of changes I've made over the years. Facing emergency surgery was a life-altering moment that once again reminded me that taking care of me on every level is as important as taking care of everyone else.

It will likely take a lot of retraining to care for ourselves the way we take care of others. Consider this a crash course to cover a few of the basic ways you can nourish your body and the way you feel in your own skin. Believe me, this crash course is way better than having a surgery be your wake-up call!

How Do I Look?

How freeing would it be to simply let go of our insecurities or the limitations of our bodies and step confidently into who we were created to be? What can we do to feel more confident in our own skin? We don't have to fit into a mold of what someone else thinks is beautiful or change simply to impress others.

Instead of asking others to weigh in on how we look, we should ask ourselves what we can do to make ourselves feel our best, most confident selves.

It's always beneficial to begin to take better care of yourself by eating cleaner, healthier food and drinking plenty of clean water. Being more mindful of what you feed yourself will result in feeling better about yourself too!

Wake Up with Makeup

As I quickly scrolled through social media today, I saw a revision of a classic inspirational message that made me giggle: *She believed she could, but she was really tired, so she didn't.*

Who hasn't felt too worn-out to do what we know we could? While clearly feeling our best, most-rested selves starts with eating good food, drinking good water, getting enough sleep, and exercising, I've found taking five minutes in the morning to put on a little strategic makeup not only makes me look as though I'm more rested, but gives me more confidence throughout the day.

Do you have an everyday, quick and natural makeup routine that makes you feel a little more awake, together, pretty, and confident?

Here are a few of my daily essentials:

- Curling my eyelashes helps lift the appearance of my eyes so I look and feel more alert!

- A quick swipe of mascara makes my eyelashes look more lush, so my eyes stand out.

- Applying a little concealer under my eyes says good-bye to dark circles.

- Filling in my eyebrows eliminates those dreaded bare spots and frames my face.

- A natural lipstick and blush makes me feel more youthful and adds a little color to my otherwise pale face.

You certainly don't need makeup to be beautiful, but I find creating a natural look with makeup helps me not only look a little livelier, but feel more confident. It's all about how you feel.

Clothe Yourself with Ease

I work from home, so I know how tempting it can be to stay in sweats. But I've found what I wear matters for my productivity level as well as how I feel about myself. Maybe you don't care about clothes, or maybe you just reason you don't have time to think about what you wear. Honestly, my goal is to put on my face and dress quickly, so I can get on with my day. I don't spend a lot of time on clothing, but I do like to wear what's reasonably current and makes me feel put together.

I feel my best when I have a few easy-to-pull-together, go-to outfits. My closet has what I used to call my "mom uniforms," but it's now more popularly called a capsule wardrobe—a few pieces that can be mixed and matched to create multiple outfits. This type of wardrobe has always worked best for me. I have a small closet, and I don't feel the need to have a lot of clothes. Plus, it cuts down on daily decisions, and for someone who struggles with being indecisive, that's a worthwhile benefit!

When your closet is set up and organized with only what you enjoy wearing, dressing with style is just as easy as throwing on sweats and a sweatshirt.

- -

5 WAYS TO DRESS FOR SUCCESS

As a stay-at-home mom and entrepreneur, I do these five things every day to feel my best:

1. *Wear actual pants.* I know! Don't roll your eyes if you're a sweatpants (or yoga pants) fan. I get that because I'm a fan too. But I've made it a point to put on real pants or even a casual dress almost every day when I'm working from home. I just feel my best, most positive self when I'm wearing actual clothes.

2. *Put on shoes.* I see a direct correlation between my shoes and my mindset. I'm not just talking about owning some cute shoes to go out in, although that's a given. I'm also talking about putting on shoes for productivity. If I'm going to go on a cleaning frenzy throughout the house, I put on my cleaning shoes. When I'm going to work from home, I put on my house shoes (not my slippers!). If I'm going to go out to meet friends for dinner, I put on my extra-cute shoes, the ones I feel most confident in! If you don't want to wear shoes in the house, get yourself a cute pair of ballerina slippers or shoes you wear only inside.

3. *Add accessories for flair.* Accessories can add pizzazz and your own signature style to even an ordinary ensemble. Adding a third piece to

your daily pants and top is an uncomplicated way to manage a pulled-together look. Every day I wear my classic wedding ring and earrings, but to feel extra put together I add a jacket or cardigan sweater and a scarf, bracelet, or necklace that completes my look.

4. *Wear colors I feel confident in.* Do you know what colors you look best in? What colors make you feel happiest and most awake? Maybe you've been told you look amazing in pink, blue, red, or black. What lifts your spirits? Add a few colorful pieces to a neutral wardrobe to brighten up your look on days when you just don't feel your best. That's what I do.

5. *Plan for a good hair day.* No one, including me, feels as if they're living their best life when they're having a bad hair day. Am I right? Get to know your hair and how to work with it. Do what you need to do to feel like a new woman. When you're feeling frumpy, ask your hairstylist to give you a new look! Whether you go longer or shorter, gray or colored or natural, embrace whatever makes you feel your very best.

Pay Attention to Your Body Language

Stand up straight to exude confidence. Put your shoulders back to feel tall and strong.

Smile, because smiling can boost your mood and make others feel at ease. It might seem like a lot of fuss and make you feel a little silly, but I suggest you practice your smile in the mirror! The language your body speaks can help you look and feel better too.

Get Healing Sleep

Do what you can to sleep better, and you will look and feel better too. Your body restores and repairs itself when it's sleeping, so aim for seven to nine hours a night.

If you have trouble falling asleep, try a diffuser with a negative ionizer and essential oils, such as lavender or cedarwood. You can even apply these oils to the soles of your feet to promote relaxation and a more restful sleep.

Use a sleep app, a sound machine, or an electric fan to lull you into a relaxed state.

Stop using your cell phone and computer right before bed! If your electronics have this option, turn their displays to "night mode" a few hours before bed because the blue lights in electronics keep us awake. Cut off all electronics for an hour or two before you need to sleep to quiet your mind. Set your phone far away from your bed at night. (This will also help you to get right out of bed in the morning when your phone alarm goes off.)

Take a hot bath before bed as a calming ritual.

Read a relaxing book before bed to quiet your mind.

Eat to Be Nourished

I'm certainly not claiming to be a food or nutrition expert, but I do know what I choose to put into my body changes how I feel. Making the effort to feed yourself well is a sign of self-love. I'll admit it took me years to reshape my perspective to reflect that mind-set, but I've seen so many positive results.

We can't control everything about our food, but we *can* learn to be more mindful and better disciplined about what we eat. Fueling our bodies with the nutrition they need to function well helps us feel better. What we eat becomes a powerful weapon against disease and contributes to healing our bodies, so the discipline of feeding your body well is a healthy lifestyle choice rather than simply a short-term diet plan.

Deciding what is the healthiest way to eat can seem overly complicated and even confusing at first, but as with most things, simplifying what we eat serves us best.

Nutrition expert and author Michael Pollan's advice in his book *Food Rules* provides this easy-to-understand framework for how to eat better: "Eat food, not too much, mostly plants...If it comes from a plant, eat it. If it was made in a plant, don't."[5]

Eating well is important to my whole family; over the years we've all made adjustments for ourselves as a matter of choice or need. We each have our own preferences, convictions, and guidelines for what we eat, but we all strive to listen to our bodies and feel healthy. As we learn more about health and what makes us feel not so good, we've altered habits, ingredients, recipes, where we shop, and where we eat.

Some members have chosen to follow a plant-based diet, and some of us are mostly vegetarian, but we've all become mindful of the food we eat. These changes didn't happen for any of us overnight, nor are they temporary. The choices we've made have become a part of how we live.

As I was writing this book I received an updated diagnosis on my own health. While I've known for years that I suffered from hypothyroidism, a new naturopathic doctor wanted to dig deeper to find the root cause. She discovered that I have Hashimoto's, a condition in which your immune system attacks your thyroid.

My health symptoms were quite nominal at the time of my diagnosis, likely a result of the accumulation of choices I've already made over the years. However, as an experiment to begin healing, she recommended that I try a completely gluten-free and mostly dairy-free diet.

A new diagnosis was just the self-care invitation I needed to get more serious about the food I ate. I had been curious about the potential impact of gluten for quite some time, but to become completely gluten-free I needed to believe it was worth the effort. I had already eliminated most dairy. Now I was convinced it was time for me to make this additional change, too. I immediately removed gluten from my diet and already am feeling better as a result. I won't be surprised at all if this becomes a permanent way of eating for me.

Once you make the commitment to a healthier diet, your perspective starts to change. None of our family feels deprived by what we don't eat. In fact, I think we enjoy eating more than ever. Real food can taste fabulous! My daughter Kylee is not only a great cook, but she discovers the best restaurants too. As we discover what food is good for us and what makes us feel our best, the temptation to eat anything else has been greatly diminished or has even vanished completely. Why eat what makes us feel yucky? We don't bring home food we shouldn't eat, and I willingly go well out of my way to eat well. I'll head to a certain coffee shop across town because they make their own alternative milk that I love.

Observing how my body reacts to food and how much better I feel when I avoid certain foods has been a key motivator to making even more changes. I still have plenty of changes I want to make, but this is a journey I'm glad to be on.

Here are a few tips I've found helpful:

- Set yourself up for success! Meal preparation is key. If you don't have delicious healthy options in the house, it's much more difficult to stay on track.

- List a few simple and manageable meals to make on those nights you just don't want to cook. Create a master list of staple ingredients on your phone or as a basis for your grocery list so you're always well stocked.

- Check each day's meal plan the night before or early in the morning so you won't feel overwhelmed at dinnertime.

- Wash and slice some carrots, peppers, or cucumbers so they'll be easy to grab during the week.

- Be mindful of what you bring in. Don't fill your cabinets with unhealthy processed snacks or junk food you'll regret eating.

- Make big batches of healthy dishes and freeze them so eating well is easy even on busy nights.

- Eat seasonally as often as possible. While we do enjoy our vegetable garden, we don't always have the time or capacity to grow everything we need. To fill our fridge with the freshest options in every season, we have a box full of organic produce grown at a local farm and green-house delivered to our door every week, all year round. We not only eat well, but this helps us try new vegetables too! We also frequent our neighborhood farmer's market. It's a fun weekend ritual and keeps us stocked with tasty food (and pretty bouquets of flowers in season).

The better you eat, the better you'll look and feel, inside and out.

 Dwell Well: Create pages in your journal for a list of your own "feel-good foods" and a list of "feel-not-so-good foods." Do you *really* feel great when you eat almost a whole bag of chips? Be honest with yourself and design your own food guidelines that truly make you feel (and look!) great. Think about a time in your life when you felt your healthiest, not necessarily your skinniest, physically. What were you eating then? What were you doing for activity?

Cook for Comfort

While you may eat food that isn't particularly good for you simply for emotional support (feeding yourself a tub of ice cream or baking a chocolate cake for a broken heart, for example), preparing good, nutritious food for yourself can be the ultimate form of self-care. Enjoy the process of cooking and knowing you're preparing a meal that will nourish your body and mind. And for your soul, say grace before the meal, offering gratitude for what has been provided and prepared for your health.

Use Your Slow Cooker

Preparing a delicious and healthy stew or soup for yourself in your slow cooker in the morning can be so comforting (and can smell divine) at the end of a long day.

Eat the Rainbow

Make preparing and eating food a visual and nutritious delight. Eating the rainbow essentially means to enjoy a variety of real fruits and vegetables (not the Lucky

Charm marshmallow rainbows!) so you receive the benefit of a balanced diet and all of the wonderful nutrients and antioxidants available.

When our children were young, we would have a good laugh over what we called our occasional "Yellow Meal." Mac n' cheese with corn on the side was a childhood favorite, but even then we realized it would have been far prettier (and undoubtedly healthier) to have at least served broccoli instead.

In spite of any earlier nutritional fails, we always taught our kids it was important to eat a variety of plant-based foods. Each member of our family loves to tell their humorous tales about the swiss chard or brussels sprouts they were introduced to at our dinner table. We've come a long way in learning how to prepare vegetables, so they are far more appealing and delicious than they were back then. Even so, serving our kids a variety of foods helped them to be in tune with healthy options and eat a more balanced diet. Maybe your children won't eat vegetables. But teaching them how to eat the rainbow can make incorporating a variety of key nutrients into their diet more fun than just eating a boring old salad.

Now that we eat so many vegetables, the variety makes our plates look prettier and more colorful than ever! To get more creative, study cookbooks and online recipes for new combinations. Try a new fruit. Switch from green grapes to red ones. And yes, buy the rainbow chard. Real food is beautiful and so good for you!

Here are just a few nutrient-rich vegetables, fruits, nuts, seeds, spices, and oils to consider incorporating into your diet:

- tomatoes
- beets
- green leafy vegetables (kale, spinach, collard greens)
- broccoli
- sprouts
- bell peppers
- cabbage
- celery
- carrots
- eggplant
- nuts (almonds and walnuts)
- olive oil
- avocados
- figs
- sweet potatoes

- fruits (pineapple, blueberries, strawberries, oranges, black-berries, grapes, cherries, goji berries, pomegranate)
- asparagus
- hemp seeds
- chia seeds
- raw apple cider vinegar
- squash
- turmeric
- ginger

Enjoy your meals as a relaxing experience. Don't just eat to frantically get to the next activity.

STAY HYDRATED

Our bodies need pure, clean water every day to function. Do whatever it takes to nourish your body well with water and keep it functioning at its peak! Get a reusable water bottle you'll use all day. Refilling it is a good a reminder to drink more. (I prefer stainless steel or glass water bottles rather than plastic.) If you have trouble drinking plain water, freeze your own fresh-fruit-infused ice cubes!

Make reminders at certain times of the day to drink water.

Drink a full glass of water before every meal.

Keep your water bottle by your bed so you can have a drink first thing in the morning.

Eat foods that are rich in water: cucumber, radishes, grapefruit, zucchini, watermelon, cauliflower, cherry tomatoes, spinach, celery, cantaloupe.

KEEP MOVING

Our bodies need regular physical activity to stay healthy. Even if you aren't a fitness buff, fit in exercise as often as possible!

- Go for a walk every morning and evening.
- Take the stairs instead of the elevator.
- Park farther away from the shopping mall or your workplace.

FULLY savor the WHOLE atmosphere surrounding a MEAL. Enjoy UNIQUE combinations of FLAVORS, textures, and SOUNDS.

- Watch a fitness video to learn proper stretching and strength training movements.

- Join an exercise class for fun and accountability.

- Count your steps every day using an app on your phone or a fitness device.

- Invest in a home treadmill, an elliptical, weights, or a bike. I have a desk-sized elliptical and a pedal exerciser that work well in small spaces!

- Find a workout buddy or goal accountability partner.

nourishing
self-care

- Find an interesting podcast or an audiobook to listen to on your morning commute instead of flipping through the same boring radio stations.

- Browse Pinterest or flip through a cookbook and save at least one healthy recipe you'd like to make. Add the ingredients to your shopping list and make it this week.

gathering

Share Your Journey

Gathering: The social act of assembling for a common purpose.

*This is the power of gathering: It inspires
us, delightfully, to be more hopeful, more joyful,
more thoughtful. In a word, more alive.*

ALICE WATERS

*The need for connection and community is primal,
as fundamental as the need for air, water, and food.*

DEAN ORNISH

W elcoming people into your home or heading out into the neighborhood
to spend quality time with others is one of the most essential aspects to
well-being. Our personality may influence how neighborly we are, or at
least will influence the frequency and how we decide to socialize.

Sometimes homebodies like myself are misunderstood. A common misconception is believing homebodies are essentially the same as hermits. That is not the case!
A hermit is someone who has withdrawn from society and lives a solitary existence.
Hermits are recluses. On the contrary, homebodies can fully love the comforts of
home and still be gracious, welcoming people. Homebodies can be well connected
to friends and family in the outside world and be delightful hosts and hostesses.

It's true, though, that the slippery slope from homebody to hermit could be a risk for some of us, particularly if we even inadvertently close ourselves off more and more from society by becoming entirely too comfortable staying home alone.

Home is the most comforting and comfortable place there is, after all.

I admit I find it rather tempting to just shut the door on a world that feels overly people-y at times. As a lover of home and all things peaceful and quiet, I often feel the world is too loud. Give me a snug little house, a fire in the fireplace, a stack of decorating books, a cozy blanket for my lap, and a hot cup of something, and I would be happy alone—for days.

But without friends, family, or a social circle for support, home would become a lonely place, even for me. We all need a community to connect to.

While we're pondering the homes, social lives, and personalities of those around us (not to be mistaken for judging or gossiping about them), making assumptions about anyone and even ourselves can often lead to unfortunate or even hurtful conclusions.

Some people mistakenly assume extroverts are intimidating, or that they don't like to be quiet or alone. Or that introverts must be sad or lonely, don't like people and therefore don't relish invitations to parties or adventures, and would never take the lead in social communities.

How unfortunate that we tend to make so many assumptions about people! The more assumptions we make, the less connected we feel to one another, and the more we miss out on what everyone brings to the table.

Like me, my son, Luke, is generally quiet, and yet he's a strong, confident person and leader. He's not shy. And, incidentally, he's a homebody who loves to travel.

As his mom, I often felt I needed to caution his teachers at the beginning of each school year about making assumptions based on his demeanor. He might have seemed like a kid who needed to be drawn out of himself to participate, but it was never long before other students were following his confident lead. (And his sophisticated humor would shine through, keeping both teachers and students laughing!)

A key difference between an introvert and extrovert is how they're energized.

Introverts become exhausted by too much social interaction; they need solitude to recharge.

Extroverts derive their energy from social interaction; they need to experience it to recharge.

Of course, there's a spectrum. A personality type with a mix of extrovert and introvert qualities is called an ambivert.

Whether we prefer a quiet or louder life, are introverted or extroverted, crave a social life on the town or in our own living rooms, we all need community to thrive.

BETTER TOGETHER

A lack of quality relationships can contribute to a decline in physical, emotional, and spiritual health. It's so important for us to feel that we belong somewhere, ideally within a circle of close friends and family, a small group, or a close community.

People these days are busier than ever. We're often connected to or distracted by electronics. We tend to spend more time apart from people than with them. But prioritizing time and energy to build community and develop healthy relationships can make a significant difference in our lives.

In her book *The Gifts of Imperfection*, Brené Brown wrote, "A deep sense of love and belonging is an irreducible need of all women, men, and children. We are biologically, cognitively, physically, and spiritually wired to love, to be loved, and to belong. When those needs are not met, we don't function as we were meant to. We break. We fall apart. We numb. We ache. We hurt others. We get sick."[1]

We're all different when it comes to how much interaction we crave and how we recharge, but all humans have an inborn need for connection and healthy relationships. In addition to providing shelter, food, and water, a sense of *belonging* to a community is one of the most important things we can create for our well-being, as well as for the health of people around us.

- Relationships get us out of our own heads (and homes) and remind us that we are part of a bigger world.

dwelling

- A variety of relationships helps expand our knowledge and perspective on life, making us more compassionate people.

- Investing in relationships provides opportunities to meet needs and become less selfish or self-absorbed.

- Building relationships offers a deep sense of purpose and fulfillment.

- Time spent in community offers many of the good things that bring joy in life; moments shared with others are often more memorable.

- Friends can be there to hold us up and lighten the load of life, and we can be there for them.

- Friends can inspire and motivate us when we're tired or have lost enthusiasm.

- A close group can produce better results for goals and offer greater well-being for everyone involved.

- More can be accomplished collectively when people gather to create, learn, improve, and refine ideas.

- A close community can keep us accountable and on the right path.

- The connections we invest in can change the course of our lives and the lives around us.

- Friends can give us a sense of security and confidence; they have our back.

- A community can be deeply united through a common experience as well as bonded by shared memories from the past.

- Friendships promote brain health and help us recover more easily from illness, loss, or hurt.

Relationships offer improved quality of life. How could you deepen a sense of belonging and connection in your life? What are some ways you could be actively investing in your current relationships or seeking a growing circle of connection?

In a world where you can be anything, be kind.
AUTHOR UNKNOWN

POSITIVE VIBES ONLY

Whom you gather with or don't gather with just might change the entire trajectory of your life. I have so many suggestions in this book for how to feel better, but the people you gather with can influence your well-being just as much as the actions you take on your own.

As they say, birds of a feather flock together, so if you have happy and positive influences in your life, you're likely to absorb those happy vibes into your life too. Gathering with people who are bettering themselves and the world around them just might be the best thing you can do for your personal well-being.

Motivational speaker Jim Rohn has said we are the average of the five people we spend the most time with. Interesting, yes? I don't think that means we ditch someone simply because they aren't like us or aren't measuring up to our standards. Not at all. It goes both ways. We need to be a voice and presence that builds up our community. We all bring something to a relationship!

What is it *you* bring to your marriage, your friendships, your community? If you're going to bring something, why not be a joy bringer?

How to make someone's day:

- Unexpectedly pay for someone's coffee or take them a coffee or tea without asking.

- Pick up a magazine or book you know your husband will love and set it on his nightstand.

- Smile and say hi to a stranger.

- Offer to run an errand for someone who's having a tough week.

- Spontaneously bake a batch of cookies and take them to a neighbor.

- Call a friend to set up a date to meet.

- Invite a friend to join you at church or to join your family for dinner.

- Leave a kind and uplifting comment on social media.

- Buy or make a yummy dinner and drop it off to an overwhelmed mom.

- Brag about someone in public who won't brag about herself.

- Keep a notebook in your purse or a note in your phone to jot down little things you discover that your friends like, and then later surprise them in some way to show you remembered.

- Text a friend a funny photo you know will make her laugh.

- Send someone a bouquet of flowers, just because.

- Simply spend quality time with someone.

- Send a spontaneous text to a friend to say hello, wish her a good day, or just to let her know you're thinking of her.

- Reminisce with someone about a funny shared experience.

- Tell your friend or spouse something you admire about them.

- Roll your neighbors' trash can back to their house after trash pick up to save them the effort.

- Respond to a harsh word with kindness.

- Compliment a stranger. You just might make a new friend.

- Write a thoughtful note and hide it somewhere a friend will find it.

Making someone's day leads to joy spreading far and wide, improved relationships, and expanding your community.

 Dwell Well: Make a list of ways you could be a joy bringer in your community, family, circle of friends, church, and so on. Write down which kinds of offerings or gestures are the most natural to the way you think, create, or interact. Let your joy bringing be an authentic expression of who you are.

BE HAPPY FOR OTHERS

I've been on all sides of belonging. I've been in the circle and out of it! Sometimes I've been popular enough to be invited into the circle, and other times I've been wallflower-ish enough to be—or at least feel—excluded. I've had seasons when I felt as though I was the center of attention and many more when I felt invisible.

For a year or two in my childhood, I was bullied by a group of kids I barely knew. That experience made me more hesitant to trust others and build relationships. For a few years after that, as a preteen, I kept mostly to myself. I felt alone, even in a big school.

Gratefully, circumstances got better as I got older, but I do think those feelings of insecurity can stay with you, particularly if you don't find a way to push past them.

I remember a situation where, even as an adult, I felt excluded. I walked into church on a Sunday morning and felt those old familiar feelings of being on the outside.

As I walked into a new-to-us church with my two little ones, I saw a circle of friends also new to me just across the lobby. They were laughing, and as I drew closer, I could tell they were chatting about a new Bible study starting that week. Not only did no one motion for me to join their circle, but I was never invited to the study either.

I tried to reassure myself that it probably wasn't intentional or personal, but of course in these situations we can feel rejected and insecure, making our minds run wild with all kinds of narratives to make sense of what's hurt us. Maybe they didn't think I had time because I was a busy young mom (none of them had children yet). Perhaps they'd decided I wouldn't be able to find childcare, or they didn't think a mom could relate to them. Perhaps they had a special bond that would have made me the oddball in the study group. Maybe their leader decided to limit the size of the group.

It's totally understandable that not everyone will be included in every group or social event, but I couldn't help but let myself wonder if I might have been left out on purpose. In all fairness, I never asked to join their group, and if I had, they may have welcomed me in with open arms! But no one wants to invite themselves into a group where they fear they don't belong.

I'll admit that, for a while, I felt a little sad watching those ladies grow closer through their connection while I was on the outside, but instead of letting myself continue to feel bummed out over it, I tried a different approach.

I decided to stop assuming how they felt about me and just let myself be happy for them.

I'm not saying being left out doesn't hurt or it's ever easy to feel like you're on the outside, but a perspective change made a difference for me personally.

Sometimes we just have to rise above feelings of rejection or envy and let ourselves *be happy for other people.* It's something I've had to do dozens of times since. As someone who has felt left out and yet has likely unintentionally made someone else feel neglected or on the outside, too, I find it helpful to assume positive intent in others.

By assuming positive intent and feeling genuinely happy that they'd found joy through their group; by not just withdrawing or nursing my wounds, feeling bitter; I felt brave enough to still welcome friendships with those same ladies outside of their group. Many of them became dear friends as we formed bonds in other ways. I'm so glad I didn't cause any relationship rifts by complicating things or acting offended.

Instead, I started looking for opportunities to be an inviter.

I made it my mission to show interest in others. I watched to see if anyone on the sidelines somewhere might be wishing they were invited in. Even if I didn't have anything to invite people to, I'd create opportunities for others to be included. I hosted movie nights, women's groups, craft nights, ladies' night outs, book clubs, Bible studies, parties, marriage groups, music practices, and mom groups.

We can broaden our circle of relationships so many ways by reaching out and inviting those who might need us to include them. Think of some ways you could become the inviter and include others in your community.

> *Friendship…is born at the moment when*
> *one man says to another "What! You too?*
> *I thought that no one but myself…"*
>
> C.S. LEWIS

BE THE INITIATOR

Have you ever considered reaching out to someone but then assumed they were probably busy, or wouldn't want their lives interrupted, or were probably doing their own thing? Maybe they were wishing they had something to do or someone to meet up with!

It takes one person to step up and create an opportunity to gather. I'm not always the brave one. Sometimes I've been too afraid of rejection or humiliation to extend an invite!

When my son, Luke, was in middle school, I noticed he wasn't invited to social events outside of school. We were relatively new to the school, and I didn't know the other parents well, so I wasn't sure if the other kids were getting together or not. But I decided to be brave and host a birthday party.

Luke wasn't too happy with me for being so brave on his behalf, but I wanted to model for him that sometimes you have to set fears aside to build community. I sent invitations to school with him, inviting all of the boys in his class to a party the last week of school. I was frankly terrified that no one would show up, but instead of making assumptions when I didn't hear from anyone on my RSVP request, I got on the phone (phone calls are not my favorite thing!) and called all the parents.

Much to my surprise, none of them were scary or mean! And every single one said yes, their son would love to come to the party. And at the party, several parents thanked me profusely for inviting their child and gathering the boys from the class. They, too, had noticed the kids didn't get together, and everyone was wondering why no one else had extended an invitation.

Who knows what might happen or who you might encourage by initiating community?

If you don't know your neighbors, you might wish you had a closer neighborhood community. What if you were the one who suggested a block party? You might be surprised to find that others had been longing for the same experience. You might just be the catalyst to forming a real community that will enhance one another's lives.

My friend Jen Schmidt wrote a book on genuine hospitality called *Just Open the Door: How One Invitation Can Change a Generation.* It's amazing what a simple invitation can do!

The key to success with inviting is following through. If you say, "We should hang out sometime!" or "We should have a neighborhood block party!" be the one who makes it happen. Make the suggestion, and then set a date and follow through.

CREATE CONNECTION POINTS

A common perception about my hometown of Seattle is that it's challenging to get to know people. It's called the Seattle Freeze. But when the sun peeks out in the Pacific Northwest, everyone heads outside. Bike riders, walkers, joggers, moms and dads with kids, teens, employees on their lunch breaks…it feels as if everyone is outside. In sunglasses, shorts, and T-shirts, with ice cream cones in hand, we're soaking in every moment of sunshine.

That's when I suddenly become more aware that people are actually friendly.

Sunshine is good for our health for many reasons, not the least of which is that it draws neighbors happily out into the community. The sun provides a common experience, and with actual eye-to-eye contact between real humans, people smile at each other again. They put away their phones (well, unless they're snapping photos to share with friends) and make actual contact with their neighbors.

Even though we all feel better in the sunshine, we don't have to wait for the right weather to connect. Our health and well-being improve if we connect to a community through every season.

My husband, Jerry, is quite neighborly. He loves connecting with people, even on gray or rainy days. He makes sure he knows people's names, he talks with everyone at grocery stores, he chats with folks at the mailbox, and he even looks around on the street to see if anyone is outside to talk to before he heads into the house. He doesn't seem to have trouble finding ways to connect with anyone.

As I've mentioned, I'm a full introvert. Although I *am* a rather private person (says the girl who's always sharing her life and home on the internet), I'm not shy or terribly awkward socially. Well, maybe I am awkward sometimes, but my point is I'm happy as a clam to be alone.

My natural inclination is to avoid social situations like the plague (as in, I run in and out of stores and make a beeline from the car to my front door, hoping no one will see me). When he first met me, my husband used to say my mysterious personality made me intriguing, so at least he reframed my inclination in a positive light.

Close friends know I'm unlikely to accept or relish an opportunity for any public appearance (but sometimes they ask anyway. I'm grateful they don't give up on me!).

I honestly have to push myself to connect with others outside of my family and my main circle of friends. This is not because I dislike people, but like a true introvert after a day of work, I'm ready to unplug from the world and refuel.

Because I don't naturally gravitate toward social interaction, over the years I have had to intentionally find or even create opportunities to invest in people and build communities.

If building relationships isn't natural for you, here are two tips that might come in handy:

1. *Show genuine interest in others.* In *How to Win Friends and Influence People*, Dale Carnegie wrote, "You can make more friends in two months by becoming interested in other people than you can in two years by trying to get other people interested in you."[2]

When you show genuine interest in other people, you'll instantly create a connection. Ask people questions about themselves to get them talking. Listening to their answers and asking more questions makes others feel valued and endeared. This may seem obvious to some, but it's not intuitive to everyone, so it's worth practicing if this is not natural for you. Asking questions is also a wonderful way for less talkative people to get to know others; you get to do less talking and more listening!

To build the relationship further, when you return home make notes about what you learned about them. The next time you expect to see your new friend, review your notes so you'll be able to pick up where you left off.

2. *Build a relationship around a common interest.* My husband and son have a great relationship, but they're different from each other in so many ways. Besides their unique personalities, many of their hobbies and interests are quite different. Nevertheless, my husband wanted a close father-son bond. Years ago, Jerry created a connection point by taking Luke to concerts and movies. Now they not only have an activity to enjoy together now that our son is an adult, but that effort built many years of memories and shared experiences throughout Luke's childhood.

When you do something new and memorable with someone, you create a special memory and opportunity to build a deeper connection.

If you don't have a common interest with anyone yet, look for ways to create one! Take lessons, join a club, visit a new restaurant in town, volunteer, plan an event, go on a trip, look for ways to create an interesting experience, or be a part of a project you can share together. Bring people together or join others around a common cause or purpose.

If you're new to an area or need to build connections from scratch, look for a local community group as a starting point:

- Join your neighborhood homeowner's association.

- Get involved in a community garden.

- Look for groups gathered around a common interest. A church or community center can be a helpful place to start your search for a group that interests you: women's groups, moms' groups, book clubs, knitting clubs, sports groups, Bible study groups, senior groups, entrepreneur groups.

- Volunteer at a church, school, retirement home, or nonprofit to get to know likeminded people.

- Join a choir.

- Go to city council meetings.

- Go to a networking event in your city.

- Attend local sporting events.

 Dwell Well: What relationship do you most want to work on right now? Journal about what hurdles you've faced before. Then list three proactive steps toward building this relationship.

HOST GATHERINGS

"Come on in and make yourself at home! I'm so glad you're here."
Aren't those the most welcoming words?

If you want to be the creator of community, you can use your home as a springboard for community and social connection. Whether you're inviting neighbors for dinner or hosting a book club, your home can be a hub for social connection!

Rest assured, your home doesn't have to be perfect to be a popular gathering place. A little imperfection can be a relief to most people! But you can do a few simple things in advance to ensure everyone feels relaxed, comfortable, and welcome.

1. *Make room to welcome guests.* Remove clutter and personal belongings around the doors where guests will enter.

2. *Create a warm environment.* Turn on lamps and, at night, your porch light for a cozy, inviting ambience.

3. *Use music.* Play pleasing background music to not only set a mood, but to fill any potentially awkward silence upon your guests' arrival.

4. *Prepare the bathroom your guests will use.* Wipe the sink and counters, scrub the toilet, and remove any laundry and personal products. Set out extra toilet paper and be sure you have enough hand soap and a clean hand towel.

5. *Have snacks and drinks ready.* Everyone feels more welcome and comfortable when they're offered food and beverages!

GATHER A COMMUNITY ONLINE

Social networking online can be an incredible opportunity to form strong relationships through similar interests, business connections, and partnerships with people, both around the country and the world. If you feel you just haven't found your people yet, believe it or not, the internet can be a great place to look for them.

While I've built many communities in real life, a lot of the friends I connect with day to day are people I've met through my computer. And, yes, I do consider them real friends. I haven't yet been able to sit face-to-face in a literal coffee shop with all of them, but I have met many in person! I still believe you need strong relationships in your everyday life, but online friendships can become just as real to me as other friendships.

The people with whom you surround yourself can inspire you to do remarkable things with your life.

Many of my online friendships have been formed through our common love of home. Through sharing about what I love, I've found others who have similar interests. It's been an amazing opportunity to gather a large community of kindred spirits.

Many people use social media as a convenient communication device to keep up with friends and family. I love seeing what my cousins are up to and staying at least somewhat connected with friends with whom I may have otherwise lost touch. Is social media a replacement for real-life connection? No. But I've found it does allow people to be less distant than they might otherwise be.

Despite downsides and even risks to our emotional well-being by becoming too involved in social media (and I don't think it's necessarily a healthy or safe place for kids to build community), establishing meaningful connections online is possible if you find a healthy community. Everyone has someplace to belong and feel supported. Just like relationship building offline, you need to choose your friendship circle wisely. It's so important to choose a community committed to building up others, but that also challenges people to think and grow in healthy ways.

Not everyone in a group has to hold the same convictions (although sometimes that's the healthiest environment for personal growth), but everyone should be respectful when they share their thoughts. In a healthy group, the atmosphere remains positive and encouraging. Mature people can agree to disagree and still be cordial.

Thousands of groups on Facebook are offered for free. Use the search bar to type in an interest and see what you find.

If you'd like to connect with my online communities, visit theinspiredroom.net/community for opportunities to find likeminded people.

GATHER YOUR FAMILY

Have you ever felt like it's a hundred times easier to gather those online friends from different states or even different countries than it is to gather the people you live with? Don't give up. With a little trial and error, you can find the gatherings that suit your family. You know the people and personalities you'll have to coax or corral, so look at this list and see—depending on the age of any children in your home—which ideas might be either a good fit or at least good inspiration to make a plan to gather soon. Don't feel the pressure to do dozens of creative activities; even a few traditions repeated often can be meaningful.

20 WAYS TO GATHER YOUR FAMILY AT HOME

1. Use conversation starter cards at dinner.

2. Make care baskets to give to a shelter or a family in need.

3. Flip through family photos and make scrapbooks.

4. Set up a tent for an indoor or backyard camping night.

5. Make your own Christmas cards.

6. Have a tea party.

7. Build a cozy blanket fort and reminisce while watching your old family movies.

8. Plan, shop for, and then prepare a meal together.

9. Have a letter-writing party. Write letters to family members or friends.

10. Dress up and have a fancy, at-home candlelight dinner.

11. Have a karaoke night.

12. Play board games.

13. Gather for brunch every Saturday!

14. Have a cupcake bake-off challenge.

15. Plant a garden.

16. Make a family summer bucket list.

17. Set up an indoor picnic.

18. Make a time capsule with special notes, memories, and letters to your future selves. Then tuck it away and set a date when you plan to open it together.

19. Film a funny family lip-synching music video.

20. Create a "build your own" party with all the toppings (ice cream bar, taco bar, waffle bar, hot chocolate bar…endless options!).

DESIGN A HEALTHY HOME FOR KIDS

The loving atmosphere we create in the home is key in the development of a strong family. We can show kids love, and model how to have healthy relationships, develop coping skills, create positive social interaction, learn manners, gain self-confidence, grow in faith and adopt values, have self-worth, care about others, and find a sense of belonging.

Home is where kids learn how to become healthy adults.

The experiences we create help prepare our children to face the world and build a healthy home for themselves. We can't control everything that happens, of course, and every kid is unique. All parents make mistakes, too, so don't beat yourself up about not getting it all right so far. Even imperfect parents can raise healthy kids. As the parents of three kids, with whom we're still very close, my husband and I did what we could to raise them to be the secure, confident, healthy adults they are today.

Making our homes a place where children feel safe and loved isn't about providing them with everything they want or offering all the warm fuzzies. It's so much more.

- It's creating boundaries for their safety.

- Sometimes it's saying no and dealing with the tantrums.

- Sometimes it's challenging them to do better because you know they'll become better for it.

- It's about simply being present rather than all the things you give them or do for them.

- It's about taking care of yourself and investing in your marriage.

- It's about modeling the behavior you want to see in them.

Did we do our jobs perfectly? No. Did we have a perfect parenting style? No. Were we perfect parents or people? No. Can we take all the credit for how awesome our children are? No.

But we did the best we could to show love, be present, and give them what they needed, even when it was hard.

DESIGN A HAPPY HOME FOR KIDS

Creating a healthy environment goes a long way toward raising happy kids. My hope is that the following ideas will help you create the healthy, happy home you envision for any children you have and who still live at home. As you read through the list, consider which ideas you've tried and which ones you might want to introduce to your crew.

- Gather at the table often.

- Establish healthy boundaries around electronics.

- Display happy family photos and mementos.

- Model healthy communication habits.

- Teach about commitment.

- Teach how to show respect.

- Teach about faith and values.

- Teach them how to take care of themselves.

- Say, "I love you."
- Say, "I'm sorry."
- Say, "I forgive you."
- Smile a lot.
- Show off their artwork or accomplishments.
- Show up to their sporting events, choir concerts, and field trips as often as you can.
- Make a list of ten things you like about them.
- Create daily routines. Children appreciate and respond well to regular, consistent routines.
- Have fun family traditions.
- Create shared experiences and memories.
- Keep the mood lighthearted. Don't escalate bad moods.
- Tuck them in at night.
- Surprise them with small treats or gifts.
- Serve others together.
- Watch family movies.
- Laugh things off when appropriate.
- Pick your battles. Not everything is a big deal.
- Create a family mission statement.
- Show hospitality and let your kids be involved.
- Say grace before meals.
- Show gratitude.
- Praise healthy and positive behavior.

- Be present in moments that matter.
- Show care for people.
- Take care of animals.
- Give hugs.

 Dwell Well: What is your definition of a healthy, happy home? Write that down in your journal and draw a border around it. Then write down any of the ideas from this section that are in line with that definition. If the list is long, choose just a couple to focus on in the coming weeks.

Through good times and bad, our family members are also our friends, and our friends are also our family members. Nothing is more satisfying than drawing the people we love together and building them up in love.

gathering
self-care

- Consider a community or circle of friends you would like to invest more time in. Plan a step forward toward building strong relationships.

- Reflect on the last time you offered an unexpected act of kindness to someone. Watch for opportunities each week. You'll likely find these kind gestures will transform your day too.

- Think about ways your dwelling could become a gathering place for others. Be open to the possibilities of meeting a need, and you'll find more community.

thriving

Trust Your New Momentum

Thriving: Prosperous and growing; flourishing.

Believe you can and you're halfway there.
THEODORE ROOSEVELT

Who am I and where am I going?

I think we all have dazed moments in this journey, perhaps as we're approaching a curve in the road where we start asking ourselves if we're going the right way. Are we fulfilling whatever it is we're here to do, or have we somehow taken a wrong turn and ended up on the wrong path?

Any uncertainty can be reminiscent of those recurring nightmares about junior high, when you can't find your locker, or you forgot to show up for a class (for the entire semester, ha!), or you panic because you've arrived at your first-period class only to discover you forgot to wear pants. Bless.

I wish the *Who am I, and why am I here, and did anyone notice I forgot my pants?* phase could be left behind along with everything else from those awkward years. We all long to feel confident, assured that our heart, head, and feet are aligned and on the right path to our one true calling.

But roads twist and seasons change. Sometimes as we come around the bend, we question ourselves or make unexpected, interesting, or even unnerving discoveries.

Whether we're beginning a new job, facing an unexpected life change, starting

Finding
our footing
wherever we are,
with a hopeful
vision for where
we're headed,
is a part
of our journey
to well-
being.

a family, watching kids leave the nest, or are simply turning 30, 40, 50, 60, 70, and beyond, we find ourselves trying to transition gracefully into the next season and embrace it.

When our kids were little, my husband and I decided one of us would be home with them as much as possible. Sometimes he was the one home while I worked, and sometimes I was at home while he worked, but doing whatever we could to be home with our kids was a commitment we both made for our family. Juggling it all was a bit hectic at times, but we had no regrets about being present at home with our kids, whether it was one of us or both of us.

As they say, you can do many things right now, in this very season in life, but you cannot do all things in every season. It can sometimes be difficult to decide which things to do, determine what to pare down, or know which battles to fight. During our childrearing season, my husband and I made sacrifices in our finances, careers, and schedules to focus on our marriage, our children, and our home.

We didn't always hit home runs, and we often blew it by biting off more than we could chew. (In spite of our priorities, life gets hectic!) But we gave it our best shot. We knew it was our one and only season for raising our kids. Eventually they would grow up, and a new season would begin for us.

Just when we think we're finally getting in our groove and comfortable in a current season, we'll hit that fork in the road that makes us reassess everything we thought we knew. If we have to turn on a road we haven't been on before, no wonder we might be unnerved. Jerry and I have found ourselves facing many forks in the road. Many of them were difficult, and we didn't always navigate well. But we all learn as we go, and if our goal is to grow, we'll find ourselves better for the journey.

Even if we're on a road we never wanted to be on, it's where we find ourselves. Will we use unplanned or unpleasant circumstances to become a *better* person or a *bitter* person? How we choose to respond to and flow with each new season we face influences our future and the people around us. We need to learn to handle every one with care.

It's easier to navigate transitions of life when we understand we were created for a purpose. Do you know why you're on this earth? Let me assure you, it isn't just to fulfill your role in a job, or to keep up on the laundry so the family has socks to wear, or to bring home a paycheck so they can spend it. (We all have to deal with wayward socks, but that's not the mission.)

We must look to the core of who we are, not the tasks we perform or the situations we experience. The tasks we do can change, life can take an unexpected turn, and we can make mistakes, but we can always grow and become stronger if we choose to bend and not break.

A new road doesn't define you; it refines you.

To experience fulfillment and authenticity, we must lean into our real purpose and embrace what we were created to do. We don't have to be defined by one season, one mistake, one set of limitations, one role or job, or one skill or talent. The twists and turns of our journey are less confusing if we remember to take an "above the clouds" perspective on everything that happens. Resting in the certainty of purpose carries us and refines us even in the difficult transitions in life. Changes help sharpen our vision and direct us to more fully embrace and become who we were designed to be.

As a Christ follower, I can be confident that my ultimate purpose is to know and serve God and to point others to Him. That mission doesn't change with what season I'm in, but how that mission is accomplished may look different in each season. I just do the best I can with what's in front of me.

Transitions can be exciting or perplexing or even scary, but they are the stretch of road we need to be on to get to the next season. Friend, if you ever find yourself in that desolate time in between, where you question who you are, you feel unsure about where you're going, or you aren't even clear on what you bring to the table anymore, remember this: You are worthy and were created for a purpose. You are unique and have much to offer.

 Dwell Well: Write your responses to these questions in your journal so you can revisit them for inspiration and guidance:

- Which priorities do you feel belong in this season of your life?

- What is it you truly want to do in this season?

- What are the passions, needs, and responsibilities you can focus on now, and which of them could wait for a future season?

WAITING EXPECTANTLY

A season of waiting—when you feel as if there are no answers or that you're going no place at all—can be either the biggest threat to your overall well-being or the most valuable season for cultivating it.

Just as cultivating soil is important preparation for the eventual health of our plants, the hard work for and anticipation of the good things to come our way result in a harvest throughout our lifetime. The waiting develops strong character and is a chance to invest in our personal well-being.

Real growth comes from *how we grow through the waiting and the season we're in*. Our well-being and that of everyone around us is affected by the mind-set we cultivate today, even *as we wait*.

Those of us who have had plenty of years and opportunities to be shaped know that waiting for the good stuff in life is hard. And wading through the hard stuff is even worse.

As kids, we're taught about the expectations and rewards of waiting. We had to wait our turn. We were expected to keep our composure and stand quietly and patiently in line when it was time to leave a classroom. Our teachers asked us to raise our hand before we were invited to speak.

At home, we had to follow the rules to reap the reward, such as an ice cream cone if we ate those disgusting veggies. On the playground, we had to wait for the other kids to finish their turn before we could take our place on the swings.

If you've ever watched a group of preschoolers waiting for anything, you've probably made a few interesting observations. Maybe you'll see the two sides of yourself too.

Kids show their emotions with actions. They might start quietly humming to themselves to pass the time and rocking back and forth, anticipating how much fun it will be to get on to the next activity. Some kids may have trouble keeping their bottom firmly planted in their seat as they raise their hand because they're so excited to have the opportunity to speak! Facial expressions often reveal their inner enthusiasm.

When a situation isn't going their way, or they're not looking forward to an experience, they often can't keep their composure. That's when we'll see those oh-so-fun toddler meltdowns. They fall on the floor wailing at the top of their lungs, legs flailing every which way!

Two of my kids would invariably have meltdowns in times of transition. The unknown was just too much. When kids are mad, they stomp their little feet and clench their hands into fists (adorable, isn't it?). They might throw something, push or yell or cry, or refuse to cooperate. They might hide so Mama can't find them.

Toddler-sized tantrums aren't fun for anyone. If we don't patiently teach them the rules or help them handle the ups and downs of life, they'll become adults who can't deal either. So we try to support our little friends in finding a more productive way to cope. We want them to gain perspective on their situation. We show them how to soothe their fear of the unknown or trust that the wait for good things is worth it. We validate their emotions and help them express how they feel with words and less drama.

You've likely observed enough toddlers to know they're just mini versions of us. They feel all of the same emotions and frustrations we do; they might just express

them a little differently. Obviously, they haven't yet had the experiences or opportunities they need to be shaped into maturity.

Lessons can be learned in every season and from every situation throughout
our entire life. Maybe you still feel as if you're prone to having toddler-like meltdowns of epic proportions when life doesn't go your way. (We're all entitled to a
few of those, right?)

We may wait with tension because we don't like how things are right now. We
may wait with anxiety and fear of what might take place. We may wait with impatience because we want to be in a different season, or with frustration when we don't
believe we have everything in place or all of the information we think we need to
move forward.

Even though waiting is hard, do we live *expectantly* for the good that's to come?
If we don't cultivate that positive perspective, we won't believe we can do anything
on our own to facilitate the growth coming our way. Expectation is participatory.
It means we believe good can always come out of something.

Highs and lows and bends in the road are a part of our stories. The lows, while
unpleasant, can signal that growth is ahead. How we live and react will either pave
the road to something beautiful or leave you feeling stuck on the side of the road.
Believing the good is still ahead will help you to round the corner with grace. Soon
this season will be behind you. As you look in the rearview mirror, you'll have more
perspective and empathy for others who are where you once were.

Dwell Well: Keep that journal open. We're doing some great
exploring in this chapter. Sit with these questions and spend
some time writing out your answers.

How can we use the situations we're in to bring light to those
around us? What can we do even now to bless others? How
can we use the wait to become better people?

*It is rare to see a life prescheduled to only 80
percent, leaving a margin for responding to
the unexpected that God sends our way.*

RICHARD SWENSON

A NEW SEASON

Have you ever walked out your front door and smelled rain in the air before
you could even see it? The year leading up to my fortieth birthday felt like that, as
if the seasons were changing and something new was on its way. (Smelling rain
before you can see it isn't only a talent Seattleites like me have. It's an actual, scientific thing!)

Change was, in fact, evolving all around me. Our son, Luke, had just entered
all-day kindergarten, and the house was unusually quiet. My girls were responsible teens and in school all day, so I had more margin in my life than ever before.

In our newly quiet house I started to sense (quite urgently, I might add) that
it was time to step out and do something new. What that would be, I had no idea.
While I believe variety can be the spice of life, I prefer to know where I'm headed
before I answer the call to a new adventure.

There's a nine-year age gap between my middle and youngest child, so as I was
approaching that fortieth birthday, I'd been living the mom season while juggling
part-time work for 18 years.

In case you're wondering why there was such a long age gap between my children, I'll go on a little rabbit trail to give you the backstory. Even though I had
always wanted to have three kids, my husband and I decided years earlier that our
two little girls had made our family wonderfully complete.

Then, as much as we enjoyed watching our daughters grow into little ladies we
knew would eventually spread their wings and fly, we realized we weren't looking
forward to being empty nesters. So, essentially, we gave ourselves an extension! We
chose to extend our young family life for another 18 years when we had our little
guy. It sounds exhausting to write it, but living it was worth it!

For many of those childrearing years, I worked for a publishing company to help make ends meet. I had a flexible schedule that allowed me to be home much of the time. Even though I didn't really want to work outside the home, it was an opportunity to be home more than not.

I loved being a mom. A wife. A homebody. I was quite content with my life as it was, so what was the new adventure stirring in me? Who was I supposed to be?

Even though I had plenty of experience to find a different job for a new or more challenging experience if I wanted to, I just wasn't interested. I was happily making a difference for the people I cared about the most, and that felt like enough. But I knew clinging to my comfort zone wouldn't help me grow, and the intensity with which I felt I was being nudged to step out in a new direction was only increasing.

That sense inside that there was something new to do made me start to question my purpose.

After a confusing year of searching, praying for answers, and long chats with my husband (who patiently tried to help me wrestle through who I was supposed to be in this next season), I discovered my answer to the restlessness inside.

Unlike how a midlife tale often plays out in the movies, in my story I didn't have to get plastic surgery or try to become someone I wasn't. The shocking reveal wasn't that I would have to leave behind everything in my homebody life for an exciting new existence, perhaps traveling the world (although if my life were a movie, I think I would have been discovered somewhere in a castle in the south of France).

No, the dramatic conclusion of that chapter in my story was that who I was, was enough. The seasons of refinement and tending to my home and family were *exactly* what qualified me for what was to come! Embracing the unknown still felt like a big, crazy leap of faith, but I had to believe that, one way or another, if I started flapping my wings, I'd learn how to fly—at 40.

Those of us who have reached the age of 40 have had to come to terms with the reality that the first 20 years of adult life are over. There is no going back! Yet look how far we've come! Beautiful things in us are just beginning to blossom and seeds can still be cultivated. We have both a story to tell and so many things we are prepared to accomplish.

No matter your age, think of all the lessons you've learned and the ways your experiences could encourage, mentor, or bless someone else. Never underestimate the power of sharing a humble, broken, or even imperfect story. Sometimes those are the most endearing and empowering stories of all.

All of the decisions you've made thus far have brought you to where you are. Don't rush to the next season or look back and feel paralyzed with regret over what's behind you. All we have is today, but what you have right now is exactly what you need to accomplish great things.

You are already qualified to be you! And that's all you need to take another step forward.

How we live each day is how we prepare for the next. It's as simple as that. Invest wisely every day. Pay attention to what stirs your heart. Nourish your soul and embrace your creativity even as you're tending to your home and your people. Everything you invest with heart and soul can be poured out to create something even more beautiful.

Dwell Well: In your journal, list opportunities you want to cultivate so you can learn something new:

- What does the delightful unknown feel like to you?
- What difficulty are you going through right now that could be redefined in your mind as a gift?

Describe your life as an adventure where the path you're on leads to unexpected joy.

DREAM BUILDING

What are your dreams? Just as it's important to nourish your body with good food, a healthy and happy vision for the future is key to your emotional well-being.

You know you're on the path that makes sense for you when you're drawing on everything within you, even on ordinary days, to create something meaningful. Not just trying to direct everyone to your highlight reel but embracing the bloopers too. Your personality and quirks, your strengths and even your limitations are a part of who you are.

Do you think the limitations you bring to the table might cancel your strengths? Do you fear the whole package of *you* doesn't seem to add up to what you need to build your dreams?

When I think about my perception of the limitations I have, I can come up short (not only because my height is short) because I start comparing them to other people's strengths. My own strong qualities might not even be everything I would choose or need, but my limitations shouldn't stop me from moving forward.

And if I don't have everything I need to follow my dreams, that just means I have areas where I can improve and ways I can grow, or opportunities to let other people shine. The limitations we have are only part of who we are. They don't define or obstruct who we can become.

Y'all, here's the thing: I don't know what "qualities" you assume everyone else has or the ones you think you're lacking, but it's the mix of who we are, the whole package from head to toe, that makes us uniquely qualified to set off on an adventure only we can live.

No one has our same style or story. No one will live life the way we can. No one can make an impact on the world the same way we will.

Trying to be like someone else or comparing ourselves to others only limits our potential. When we draw on everything in us and around us, it's as if we find our own secret sauce. That's where the magic is—what you have within you and around you are the exact tools you'll need to build the dreams waiting for you.

How can any of us fulfill our own purpose or achieve dreams if we're masquerading as someone else, anyway? What good would come of it if I tried to fool you into believing I'm a rocket scientist? I'm clearly not a rocket scientist, even if I try to make you think I am. I'm still just me, the same homebody, sitting here on my couch in my living room.

When you embrace everything you are as you build your dreams, the sky's the limit for what you can do to seize the adventure of your life! Sure, you'll have things to figure out. Questions you'll need to ask. Answers you'll need to uncover. New skills to acquire. Lessons still to be learned, and a continual refining of your character in the process. Each season will bring fresh opportunities to grow or pursue your dreams in a new way.

Young moms often ask me how I find time and energy to do all of the things I do today. Remember, I'm in a different season than I once was. These days those toddlers I used to chase are now running with me to build our dreams. They still keep me on my toes, but they also carry more of the load.

Believe me, Mama, your littles will grow up too. You'll not only be amazed at what your children can do someday, but you'll be surprised at all you'll be able to do!

Your dreams don't have to wait for someday. There is a season for everything, but you can invest in your dreams in every one of them. I was passionately learning and growing my skills even as a young mom. I just didn't know at the time how they would eventually grow or blossom as the years went on. Embrace the season you're in and be diligent in the opportunities you have in front of you today.

You don't have to have everything all figured out to start building dreams. You don't have to have all of the answers about the future to take a step. When I first started my business at age 40, I literally had no idea what I was doing, how to do it, or where I was headed.

I didn't have a degree in English, design, or business. No instruction manual for what I was supposed to do immediately existed, let alone for what I was expected to do later. It was a figure-it-out-as-you-go kind of deal. I simply had to learn to be a "can do" person rather than a "can not" person.

Our minds are powerful. The thoughts we have about ourselves, the very words we speak to ourselves, can become the reality we believe. If you believe you are capable, you'll become capable. If you tell yourself you don't have what it takes, you'll believe it, and that will be the end of the story.

I love how life coach Marie Forleo puts this into perspective: "Everything is figureoutable."

When you embrace your own path, the beauty you have to offer can begin to bloom and grow. If you're ready to experience a holistic mind-set of greater well-being, it will start to become evident from the inside out. Your thoughts start to change. You become deeply committed to doing what it takes to become the kind of person you want to be. You'll start looking for ways to learn and grow rather than focusing on all the reasons you think you can't.

Maybe you're feeling stirred to leave the comforts of home or your current job to begin a new adventure, but you aren't sure what that means. Why don't you lean into that dream for a bit? Don't automatically shut it down with a list of reasons why not. Let your mind ponder in a fresh direction.

 Dwell Well: Grab your journal and turn to a new page. It's time to start a new chapter. Write "Dream Building" at the top. We're not just fantasizing about some sort of impossible feat when we put words and ideas to paper. We're searching for vision and ways to shape our future. We're reminding ourselves that nothing is impossible, so don't write out limitations or the why nots. It's time to explore the what-ifs.

- What stirs your heart and ignites your passion?
- If you could do anything with your life, hobby, or career, what would you love to do? It doesn't have to be big. It can be as simple as how my own dream began, to fully embrace my calling as a homebody.
- If you're already doing what you love, perhaps you're ready for some refinement or even the next step. As we grow, our perspective and even direction can change. We don't have to keep doing what we've always done, so this might be a season where you redesign what you do.
- Describe your very best life. Where do you live there? What do you do every day?
- Consider the life you'd love to live sometime in the future.
- Picture your life in three years. What would you love to be doing? Ideally, how would you spend your time? Be as detailed as possible. How would you feel?

Even if you're not sure what you would want your life to look like, use your journal to start dreaming.

What season of life are you in right now? Describe it and what you're doing right now to invest in your everyday, ordinary life. Be aware of this season as an extraordinary one. It's where you're developing your skills, discovering your passions, and nurturing your mind-set.

*Find what makes your heart sing
and create your own music.*
MAC ANDERSON

THE DELIGHTFUL UNKNOWN

> Now I understand that in order to feel a true sense of belonging, I need to bring the real me to the table, and that I can only do that if I'm practicing self-love. For years I thought it was the other way around: I'll do whatever it takes to fit in, I'll feel accepted, and that will make me like myself better. Just typing those words and thinking about how many years I spent living that way makes me weary. No wonder I was tired for so long! (Brené Brown, *The Gifts of Imperfection*).

How often do we dismiss or even feel paralyzed by the potential beauty of what our life could be?

My grandma designed the most stunning garden outside her ground-level apartment. When she moved in, just beyond her patio doors was a small but barren corner hillside. Her neighbors dismissed making something of that north-facing space as too daunting, considering it unsuitable for growing anything at all. But she didn't look at what was; she saw possibilities. Her vision, tenacity, and determination to create something beautiful there eventually proved the neighbors wrong!

Over the years, as she cultivated the soil and tended to her garden, colorful flowers and exquisite foliage emerged, surprising everyone who passed by. Her daily TLC brought life to that space. I still drive by that corner and find delight in her example, a reflection of what can be just ahead when we're open to possibilities. If we press forward into the growth that first must take place within us, trusting in the process, something beautiful emerges.

Gertrude Jekyll, a famous British artist and horticulturist, was advised by her doctors to give up painting in her late forties because her eyesight was growing increasingly poor. Instead of mourning the loss of a creative outlet, she applied her creative spirit to what became her most well-known careers—as a garden designer and author.

> Let no one be discouraged by the thought of how much there is to learn. Looking back upon nearly thirty years of gardening (the

earlier part of it groping ignorance with scant means of help), I can remember no part of it that was not full of pleasure and encouragement. For the first steps are steps into a delightful unknown, the first successes are victories all the happier for being scarcely expected, and with the growing knowledge comes the widening outlook, and the comforting sense of an ever-increasing gain of critical appreciation. Each new step becomes a little surer, and each new grasp a little firmer, till, little by little, comes the power of intelligent combination, the nearest thing we can know to the mighty force of creation.[1]

I don't know about you, but at first glance, stepping into the unknown sounds anything but delightful to me. It feels scary, and I don't like surprises. It can be unnerving to figure out how to move forward with grace and confidence through the unexpectedness of life.

Even though the path ahead won't be revealed to us until the proper time, moving forward anyway is how we learn to live more fully with what we've been given.

Return to this question from the start of our journey as you go through your days and face new opportunities for growth: What action could you take to feel more balanced, to find greater wellness and peace in how you live?

We must take a step in the direction we think is right and do whatever we know to do right now, believing the journey is where the real growth takes place. As we learn more, each step becomes a little surer. We see how beauty begins to emerge from barren ground around us, each new corner revealing a wider vision of our own purpose in this world.

So many life lessons can be learned from a garden. Growth in our well-being happens when we make mindful progress toward tending to it every day. It's the result of putting feet on the ground, hands in the dirt, weeding out what isn't beneficial and tending to what matters to our health.

This runs counter to this sped-up, hurry-along, impatient society we live in. Trying to keep up with the constant need for consumption and information sets a pace that ultimately doesn't fill us; it just wears us down. Well-being is found through the slow nurturing of all we are and an investment in who we're becoming. It's in tending well to our needs and our dwellings—home, body, mind, and spirit.

What if, going forward, we intentionally left more space in our schedules? When you look at the information tag on a shrub you want to plant in a garden, you'll notice the instructions suggest you leave a certain amount of space around the plant so it has room to grow. We have more room to grow in unscheduled and unhurried moments. Being okay with quiet inspires us to trust, listen, and contemplate our next steps rather than continue to run in circles.

When our schedules are always filled to the brim with busyness and activities that aren't meaningful to us fill even our downtime, what are we so busy with? Is our constant activity in line with who we want to be? Our time is precious and valuable. Minutes and hours and days add up to our life.

Well-being can grow in the margins we guarded for the beautiful unexpected in our life to unfold. We need time to explore creativity and curiosity. A frantic pace stifles us from experiencing the abundant life we're meant to *discover*.

If we really want to live a full, rewarding, vibrant, and meaningful life, one that can continue to grow and blossom in the seasons to come, what can we do to plant the seeds today? How can we slow down to cultivate the soil, so our days start to reflect our true passions?

We may not yet fully see how the seeds we plant in this season are preparing to grow and blossom in a future season, but the root of our well-being stems from the life we choose to cultivate with all that we have right now.

> *Far better is it to dare mighty things, to win glorious*
> *triumphs, even though checkered by failure...*
> *than to rank with those poor spirits who neither*
> *enjoy nor suffer much, because they live in a gray*
> *twilight that knows not victory nor defeat.*
>
> THEODORE ROOSEVELT

Our well-being flourishes best when it's nurtured like a well-tended garden. It thrives with seasons of rest, renewal, growth, and harvest.

Each season is a new opportunity to grow in our potential, to be well in all areas of our life, to transform us from the inside out. When we find meaning and purpose in nurturing what is right in front of us, we not only find a state of well-being improves our own lives, but changes the world around us.

How we spend our days is, of course, how we spend our lives.
ANNIE DILLARD

thriving
self-care

Answer these questions in your journal:

- Who are you at your core, and how can you invest what you have right now in becoming everything you were created to be?

- How can you make the most of your current situation and season? What joy and blessings are already in front of you?

- Do you live out your life purpose with great intention, looking forward with anticipation to the possibilities still ahead?

final thoughts

Dear friend, our time here is coming to a close. As I shared when we began this journey together, feeling well where you dwell isn't about achieving perfection in your home or body. Dwelling well is about embracing the art of caring for yourself and your surroundings, even in small but meaningful ways.

Before you turn this last page, I encourage you to highlight the self-care reminders and Dwell Well questions that speak to your journey now.

If you will spend some time journaling about those, that will serve you well in the days and years to come. The practice of writing your thoughts, insights, and questions can continue to be therapeutic and productive! Revisit your notes often to see how far you've come as well as to be mindful of ways you can always treat yourself better. Your insights will remind you to grow in grace, understanding, and knowledge.

I hope we'll stay in touch!

Be well,

Melissa

notes

Chapter 1: invitation

Epigraph: Invitation—Cambridge Dictionary, https://dictionary.cambridge.org/us/dictionary/english/invitation.

Chapter 2: well-being

Epigraph: Well-being—English Oxford Living Dictionaries, https://en.oxforddictionaries.com/definition/us/well-being.

Epigraph: Wellness—National Wellness Institute, https://www.nationalwellness.org/page/AboutWellness.

Chapter 3: sanctuary

Epigraph: Sanctuary—Your Dictionary, http://www.yourdictionary.com/sanctuary.

Chapter 4: loveliness

Epigraph: Loveliness—Dictionary.com, https://www.dictionary.com/browse/loveliness.

Chapter 5: savoring

Epigraph: Savoring—Merriam-Webster, https://www.merriam-webster.com/dictionary/savor.

Chapter 6: streamlining

Epigraph: Streamlining—Merriam-Webster, https://www.merriam-webster.com/dictionary/streamline.

Chapter 7: foraging

Epigraph: Foraging—Paraphrased from Dictionary.com, https://www.dictionary.com/browse/foraging.

1. ScienceDirect, "The influence of urban green environments on stress-relief measures: A field experiment," June 2014, https://www.sciencedirect.com/science/article/pii/S0272494413000959?via%3Dihub.

2. "Bergamot (Citrus bergamia) Essential Oil Inhalation Improves Positive Feelings in the Waiting Room of a Mental Health Treatment Center: A Pilot Study," March 24, 2017, https://www.ncbi.nlm.nih.gov/pmc/articles/PMC5434918/.

Chapter 8: nourishing

Epigraph: Nourish—Dictionary.com, https://www.dictionary.com/browse/nourishing?s=t.

1. Brother Lawrence, *The Practice of the Presence of God* (New Kensington, PA: Whitaker House, 1982), first conversation.

2. Lawrence, *The Practice of the Presence of God,* ninth letter.

3. Brother Lawrence, *The Practice of the Presence of God* (Old Tappan, NJ: Fleming H. Revell Company, 1967), fifth and seventh letters.

4. Brother Lawrence, *The Practice of the Presence of God* (New Kensington, PA: Whitaker House, 1982), twelfth and thirteenth letters.

5. Michael Pollan, *Food Rules* (New York, NY: Penguin, 2009), xv.

Chapter 9: gathering

Epigraph: Gathering—Vocabulary.com, https://www.vocabulary.com/dictionary/coming%20together.

1. Brené Brown, *The Gifts of Imperfection* (Center City, MN: Hazelden Publishing, 2010), 26.

2. Dale Carnegie, *How to Win Friends and Influence People* (New York, NY: Simon and Schuster, Inc., 2010), 52.

Chapter 10: thriving

Epigraph: Thriving— English Oxford Living Dictionaries, https://en.oxforddictionaries.com/definition/thriving.

1. Gertrude Jekyll, *Wood and Garden* (London, New York, and Bombay: Longmans, Green and Co., 1899), 5.

about the author

Melissa Michaels is a *New York Times* bestselling author and creator of *The Inspired Room*, an award-winning blog that has been one of the top home decorating destinations on the web for more than 11 years. She lives in Seattle with her husband, Jerry; their teen son, Luke; and adorable doodle pups Jack and Lily. The Michaels' two grown daughters, Kylee and Courtney, are a key part of the creative team at *The Inspired Room*.

You can connect with Melissa and find her blog, social medial channels, and community at **theinspiredroom.net/community**.

Visit **DwellingBook.com** for related resources, downloadable images, and more.

To learn more about Harvest House books and
to read sample chapters, visit our website:

www.harvesthousepublishers.com

HARVEST HOUSE PUBLISHERS
EUGENE, OREGON